# AMERICA'S REIGN OF TERROR

### World War I, the Red Scare, and the Palmer Raids

*A knock on the door in the middle of the night . . .
Arrest without warrant . . . Jail without charges . . .
Twenty years in prison for Americans who disagreed with
the President's war policy . . . Aliens herded aboard
ship and sent back where they came from . . . Lynching, looting, and rioting . . . .*

*This was America between 1917 and 1920, when the
worst possible crime was to dissent—or to be different.*

*illustrated with photographs*

# AMERICA'S REIGN OF TERROR

World War I, the Red Scare, and the Palmer Raids

## by Roberta Strauss Feuerlicht

*Foreword by Norman Dorsen*

RANDOM HOUSE · NEW YORK

In memory of my mother

# Lena Wesler Strauss

1896–1969

*"Her children rise up and call her blessed."*

Proverbs (31:28)

PICTURE CREDITS: Boston Globe: 112; Brown Brothers: cover, 52–53, 57, 70–71, 77, 107, 110; Culver Pictures: 34, 41, 84, 88; Historical Pictures Service, Chicago: 11, 30, 61, 65, 105; Library of Congress: 24, 89; National Archives: 17; United Press International: ii, 4, 13, 94, 97.

# Foreword

This book vividly describes an important but often neglected chapter in American history. It is not a pretty story. War usually breeds excesses, domestic as well as foreign, and World War I was no exception. As usual, the chief victims were the strangers within the gates—the aliens, radicals, minorities and dissenters.

In the perspective of half a century there may be some who feel that there was no real "terror," and that—given the jingoism of the man in the street—the nation was as close to normal as wartime conditions would permit.

It is true that the fear abroad in the land was concentrated among a relatively small portion of the population, and was not accompanied by prolonged physical oppression—for example, of the kind that has been visited upon black citizens in many parts of the country.

But terror is not just a body count. Terror exists when a person can be sentenced to years in prison for an idle remark; when people are pulled out of their beds and arrested; when 4,000 persons are seized in a single night; and when arrests and searches are made without warrants. Moreover, for each person sent to prison for his views, many others were silenced. The author amply documents the government's insensitivity to civil liberties during this period, its frequent brutality and callousness, and the personal grief that ensued.

The period of the Palmer Raids should be pondered as an example of the worst in American history. This book, if taken to heart, will be an eloquent warning to all, especially in times of crisis.

NORMAN DORSEN

*New York University School of Law*

# CONTENTS

# Prologue

*If . . . some of my agents out in the field . . . were a little rough and unkind, or short and curt, with these alien agitators . . . I think it might well be overlooked.*

Attorney General A. Mitchell Palmer

On Friday evening, November 7, 1919, federal agents and New York city police and detectives packed themselves into a group of automobiles. Swiftly, the convoy drove to the Russian People's House at 133 East 15th Street. One by one the cars quietly parked on nearby side streets so no one would be warned of their coming. Then the police and agents climbed out of the automobiles, surrounded the building, and burst in.

One room of the Russian People's House served as the office for a radical organization called the Union of Russian Workers. In the other rooms, classes were held for Russian immigrants. They learned English, mathematics, mechanics, and other skills that would help them become better Americans.

Some 200 men and women were in the building when the raid began. They did not know about it until a voice shouted, "Out into the hall, everybody! Line up there and don't make any noise!"

The bewildered immigrants huddled in the hallways. Many of them could barely understand English. Finally one woman asked what was happening. "Shut up there you, if you know what's good for you," was the reply.

Not everyone in the building heard the order to

line up in the hall. Fifty-year-old Mitchel Lavrowsky was teaching algebra and Russian in a room on the second floor when several agents entered. One of them pointed a gun at Lavrowsky and ordered him to remove his glasses. When he did the agent struck him over the head.

Lavrowsky was beaten by three agents. By then, too weak to walk, he was thrown down the staircase. Spaced along the steps were other federal agents and city police, armed with blocks of wood ripped from the banister. As Lavrowsky rolled between them they beat him again.

At the bottom of the stairs Lavrowsky was ordered to wash away the blood so reporters waiting outside would not see it. Then he was taken by car to the New York office of the Department of Justice at 13 Park Row to be questioned.

Since he was completely innocent of any crime he was released at midnight. His head, left shoulder, and left foot were broken.

Semeon E. Kravchuck was on his way to class that evening when he was stopped on the street by a plainclothesman and ordered into the Russian People's House. There he was beaten on the head and body and a tooth was knocked out. After questioning at the Park Row office he was released.

A passerby, Peter Karas, happened to be walking on East 15th Street at the time of the raid. Two federal agents stopped him, struck him, and hauled him in for questioning. He too was released.

The police and federal agents worked rapidly. The raid began at about 8 P.M. Within an hour everyone in sight had been taken to Park Row for questioning. Many had their heads wrapped in bandages.

While the arrests were being made, the raiders were also busily breaking up the building. A *New York Times* reporter described the scene. "Doors were taken off," he wrote, "desks were ripped open, and even the few carpets were torn up to find possible hiding places for documents."

New York was not the only place where the Justice Department struck that weekend. On Friday evening and Saturday, federal agents and local police made raids in at least 15 cities. They were looking for members of the Union of Russian Workers, whom they considered to be dangerous aliens. But it was sometimes hard to tell who was more dangerous, the aliens or the agents.

In Bridgeport, Connecticut, a group of 63 Russian immigrants happened to meet that Saturday to discuss buying a car. They wanted to use it to learn how to be auto mechanics.

The raiders swooped in and arrested them all. One of the immigrants was a machinist named Semeon Nakhwat. He later testified, "I am not an anarchist, Socialist, or Bolshevik and do not take much interest in political theories." Like many other immigrants he had joined the Union of Russian Workers in order to study in their classes and have other Russians to talk to.

*Broken furniture, smashed typewriters, ripped documents— the office of a radical organization after a raid in November 1919.*

Nakhwat was held in jail for six weeks before he was even granted a hearing. After questioning he was returned to jail. Six weeks later he was questioned again. A federal agent asked him for the address of a suspect who lived in Brooklyn. Nakhwat said he didn't know the man. The agent struck him in the face. When Nakhwat fell to the floor, the agent kicked him in the back.

Later, Nakhwat was put in a special punishment chamber in the basement of the jail. It was a tiny, dark room built over a boiler. The heat was almost unbearable.

Nakhwat was kept in the room for 36 hours. During that time he was twice given one piece of bread and one glass of water.

When a lawyer became interested in Nakhwat's case, he was released on bail. He had spent five months in jail without being charged with any crime.

The arrests and treatment of prisoners followed the same pattern all across the country. In Detroit, Alexander Bukowetsky and 13 other men were seized at a concert given by the Union of Russian Workers. They were not permitted to notify their families, who had no idea why they had disappeared.

After being questioned and beaten, Bukowetsky was transferred to several different jails. By now four months had passed, and his wife knew where he was. One day she came to visit him with their two children, 12-year-old Violet and 4-year-old Robert.

A police inspector said to Mrs. Bukowetsky, "Did you come here to make trouble again?"

"Why, no," she replied. "I just came to see my husband."

"If you talk back like that," snapped the inspector, "get out!"

"I won't get out until I see my husband," she said.

A guard summoned Bukowetsky. When he came in, another guard hit his wife in the chest with a gun, knocking her to the floor. When Bukowetsky tried to shield her with his body, several guards began to beat him.

"Please don't hurt my father and mother," Violet begged. But the guards continued to hammer at their victims.

Most of the persons seized in the November raids were finally released for lack of evidence. In New York, 150 of some 200 arrested were freed within two days. A reporter noted that "most of them . . . had blackened eyes and lacerated scalps."

The raids had victimized a great number of innocent men and women. But the Attorney General of the United States, A. Mitchell Palmer, said he was pleased. Someone in his office announced that the raids were "the first big step to rid the country of . . . foreign trouble makers."

Meanwhile, Alexander Bukowetsky sat in his cell with three holes in his head. He wrote sadly, "When I came to America I came with the thought that I was coming to a free country,—a place of freedom and happiness, and I was anxious to come. . . . As much as I was anxious to come here to America I am a hundred times more anxious to run away from Americanism."

For Bukowetsky and others the American dream of democracy had died. In its place there had risen the nightmare of a Reign of Terror.

## 1

# The War to End War

*The whole damn war's crooked from start to finish.*

John Dos Passos, THE 42ND PARALLEL

The Terror did not begin on a single day nor did it spring from a single cause. History is never quite that simple. The Terror festered and grew because problems that had been simmering in America for many years were brought to a boil by the flames of a vast European war.

World War I began in a place few Americans had ever heard of and fewer still could pronounce. It was a distant city called Sarajevo, which is the capital of Bosnia. Today, Bosnia is part of Yugoslavia. In 1914 it was a province of the Austro-Hungarian Empire.

Many Bosnians wanted to be free of Austria. But a conquered people cannot vote their rulers out of office. A group of Bosnian youths decided their only weapon was assassination. They decided to kill Archduke Franz Ferdinand, the heir to the Austrian throne, hoping to spark a rebellion in Bosnia.

The young men who plotted against Franz Ferdinand were idealists, but an idealist with a gun in his hand is a potential murderer. On June 28, 1914, Franz Ferdinand made an official visit to Sarajevo. He was shot to death by 19-year-old Gavrilo Princip.

The assassination of Franz Ferdinand did not raise

a rebellion in Bosnia but it did trigger World War I. Most of the statesmen of Europe did not really want war, but they had their faces to save. So they gave way to their generals, who did want war because it was the only occupation they knew.

On one side of the war were the Central Powers— Germany and Austria. On the other side were the Allies—England, France, and Russia. A number of smaller nations were drawn in as well.

At first, Americans were puzzled. They could not understand what had led Europe to the slaughter or what any country hoped to gain. Even America's leading hawk, former President Theodore Roosevelt, couldn't decide which side he was on. He called on the nation to be "entirely neutral" and wrote, "It would be folly to jump into the gulf ourselves to no good purpose."

Almost all Americans wanted to be neutral in deed, which meant staying out of the war. But they were not neutral in thought. A majority sympathized with the Allies. Although all the major European powers were partially responsible for the war, the greatest guilt fell on Germany and Austria. Besides, both of these countries were ruled by monarchs, while France and England were democracies. Some Americans saw the war as a struggle between good and evil, democracy and dictatorship.

But Germany also had American sympathizers. The largest group of immigrants in America were of German descent. Another large group, the Irish, hated England because of her persecution of Ireland.

Those who favored the Central Powers could also argue that the democracies, England and France, were allied with Russia, which had the most oppressive government in Europe.

Two weeks after the war began in August 1914, President Woodrow Wilson asked Americans to be neutral in thought as well as action. But Wilson was neutral on the side of the Allies. He permitted American businessmen to sell them food, supplies, and weapons. When the Allies ran out of money, Wilson permitted American bankers to lend them more.

The President went even farther. England used her gigantic fleet to blockade European ports so no supplies could reach the Central Powers. It meant that America could not trade with Germany or Austria all the while she was supplying arms and materials to the Allies. Yet Wilson protested only mildly.

Germany did not think this was very neutral. She set up a submarine blockade to sink ships carrying supplies to England. At this President Wilson protested vigorously, and Germany backed down.

As the war went on, American sentiment swung more and more to the Allies. Theodore Roosevelt, who thought war was "great fun," wanted to lead a division in this one. He now urged Wilson to join the Allies. When Wilson refused, Roosevelt called him a "coward."

If hawks like Roosevelt could not get America into the war at once, they could at least prepare her for it. There arose a loud clamor that America build up her arms and armed forces.

The preparedness campaign was led by Republicans representing two streams that often flow together in wartime. One was the mindless patriotism that demands that America enter and win every battle, anywhere in the world. The other was greed. There were many corporations that would make fortunes manufacturing and selling war supplies.

At first President Wilson resisted the preparedness drive. But he was a Democrat, who had to run for reelection in 1916. Fearing the Republicans would accuse him of weakening America, he seized the preparedness issue and made it his own.

Congress passed the preparedness program under heavy pressure from the President. The size of the army was to be doubled, and a huge fleet of warships was to be built.

But even while America was arming for war, Woodrow Wilson still wanted to be peacemaker to the world. As the trenches of Europe filled with mud and blood he offered his services to both sides. But neither really wanted peace except on its own impossible terms.

When Wilson ran for a second term as President in 1916, peace sentiment in America was overwhelming. He won the election with the slogan, "He kept us out of war." In one speech he asked, "Have you heard what started the present war? If you have, I wish you would publish it, because nobody else has, so far as I can gather." In another speech he said, "I am not expecting this country to get into war."

But he was wrong. By the end of the year Germany

*A World War I trench during the Battle of the Somme, in which more than a million men were killed or wounded. Wrote a French lieutenant: "Hell cannot be so terrible."*

had made an important decision. Publicly she offered to negotiate peace. Privately she decided that if the offer was refused she would end the war swiftly by resuming submarine warfare. Her submarines would sink all ships carrying supplies to England even if this meant bringing America into the war.

The Allies rejected the German peace offer. Soon after, Germany announced that her submarines would attack all ships found in Allied waters.

America was stunned. For two and one-half years

she had been growing fat on Allied war orders. If trade with the Allies ceased, there would be an economic disaster. Businesses would fail. People would be thrown out of work.

President Wilson broke off diplomatic relations with Germany. But he still hoped to avoid war, which most Americans opposed. Then, at the end of February 1917, he learned that the Germans had invited Mexico to join them if Germany went to war with America. In return Germany promised Mexico most of the southwestern United States.

Wilson was furious. He used this information to help make Americans angry enough to fight Germany. Most Americans forgot, or did not know, that the area in question had been taken from Mexico by force. Besides, the Allies had also drawn small nations into the war on their side by promising them someone else's territory.

On March 18, while America was still seething over the German offer to Mexico, German submarines sank three American merchant ships. At about the same time came the first phase of the Russian Revolution. The Tsar was forced from power and liberals formed a new government. The Allies no longer suffered the embarrassment of having the worst ruler in Europe on their side.

For the next two weeks America hovered between peace and war. The majority of Americans still favored peace—but President Wilson was no longer among them.

No one can be certain why Wilson decided to go to war. During the critical weeks when he was making up his mind, he received word that the Allies were losing, and only American intervention could save them. He was also outraged by the German attacks on American shipping, though it is not clear why he should have expected Germany to continue to permit America to supply and finance the Allies.

Whatever his reasons were, it was typical of Wilson that his decision to enter the war was stated in terms of high moral purpose. On April 2, 1917, the President asked Congress for a declaration of war against the Central Powers. He said America would be

*April 2, 1917: President Woodrow Wilson asks Congress for a declaration of war. "It is a fearful thing to lead this great peaceful people into war," he said.*

fighting to make the world "safe for democracy."

War was declared on April 6. Six senators and 50 representatives voted against the resolution. They were among those Americans who believed that, no matter what Wilson said or thought, the causes of the war were more economic than idealistic. They felt America was protecting not democracy but the bankers who had loaned the Allies over $2 billion. "We are going into war upon the command of gold," said Senator George Norris of Nebraska.

Many people agreed with Senator Norris in 1917, and many still believe that America entered World War I mostly for economic reasons. Half a century after the war, British historian A. J. P. Taylor would write, "If the German submarines stopped . . . trade, there would be depression, crisis. If the Allies lost the war, the American loans would be lost also.

"In the last resort, the United States went to war so that America could remain prosperous and rich Americans could grow richer."

2

# Words at War

*Was not war in the interest of democracy for the salvation of civilization a contradiction in terms?*

Jane Addams

In 1937 a national polltaker asked Americans, "Do

you think it was a mistake for the United States to enter the [first] World War?" Seventy percent, or nearly three out of four, replied, "Yes." The figure would not have been as high in 1917, but Woodrow Wilson did lead America into war unsupported by a majority of the people.

For over two and one-half years Americans had been told by various leaders, including the President, that they should be neutral. Wilson had said he didn't know the war's causes or its aims. He had just been reelected because "He kept us out of war." Yet one month after being sworn to a second term he had turned himself around. Now his problem was to turn the country around with him.

One of Wilson's enemies once called him "a man of high ideals but no principles." He was a dour, thin-lipped man who cared about ideas rather than people. His father was a minister, and there was a good deal of preacher in the President as well.

America had less reason for going to war than any other combatant, so Wilson had to find one to suit his conscience. It could no longer be just another war but a war to end war, a war to make the world safe for democracy. Wars are dirty but crusades are holy, so Wilson turned the war into a crusade. Other nations might fight for power or possessions; America would fight to build a better world.

Once Wilson preached his crusade he expected everyone to rise up and follow him. He was the sort of man who simply could not bear opposition on matters of conscience. If he said World War I was right, then it was right. People who disagreed with him were either misinformed or disloyal. If they were misinformed they could be corrected. If they were disloyal they had to be punished.

First, Wilson dealt with the misinformed. A week after America entered the war he created the Committee on Public Information (CPI). Its chairman was a journalist named George Creel. The purpose of the CPI, said Creel, was to win the "hearts and minds" of the American people.

The CPI was a massive exercise in thought control. It bombarded Americans with Wilson's view of the war until it became their view as well.

In 1917 there was neither radio nor television for the CPI to use. But every other channel of communication was choked with government news and propaganda.

When an American read his newspaper he read the same CPI-approved war news no matter where he lived or what newspaper he bought. If he was an immigrant who didn't understand English he read the same story translated for the foreign-language newspaper of his choice.

If he belonged to a men's club he would hear CPI speakers at its meetings. If his wife belonged to a women's club she learned through another division of the CPI how she could help win the war.

When their children went to school they saw war photographs issued by the CPI and recited patriotic poems written by CPI poets. Their lessons in current events were given by teachers using CPI materials.

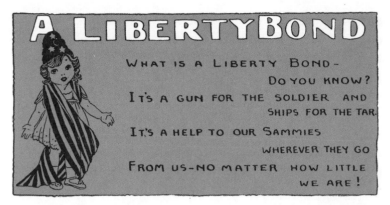

A LIBERTY BOND

WHAT IS A LIBERTY BOND—
DO YOU KNOW?
IT'S A GUN FOR THE SOLDIER AND
SHIPS FOR THE TAR.
IT'S A HELP TO OUR SAMMIES
WHEREVER THEY GO
FROM US—NO MATTER HOW LITTLE
WE ARE!

*No one was too young to escape CPI propaganda. This jingle taught toddlers about Liberty Bonds, which the government sold to help pay for the war.*

If the members of the family went to a movie at night they saw war cartoons produced by the CPI or heard a man deliver a four-minute CPI speech on why America had to win. If they went to church on Sunday they heard their preacher deliver blessings and prayers written for him by the CPI.

The CPI flooded the country with patriotic posters, buttons, and stickers. It even prepared pamphlets for traveling salesmen to hand out with their wares as they went from town to town.

All of the CPI propaganda had but one aim. It had to make the war seem worth dying for. It proclaimed that a German victory would mean the end of civilization. An American victory would not only save democracy but bring eternal peace.

The drumbeat of patriotic propaganda on the eyes,

ears, and nerves of the American people soon had its desired effect. The majority were changed from cautious doubters to true believers. Everything American became beautiful and good. Everything German became sinister and hateful.

But for all the pounding propaganda of the CPI, several groups resisted its call. One was made up of isolationists who felt that no European quarrel was any business of theirs.

The second was made up of immigrants—mostly German and Irish—who had good reason to hate England more than Germany.

A third category consisted of pacifists and progressives. Most of them were either journalists, professors, ministers, or social workers like Jane Addams.

In 1889, Jane Addams had founded Hull House in the slums of Chicago. It was a settlement house, a place where the neighborhood poor could go to learn and to relax.

Working at Hull House, Jane Addams learned that the poor needed justice, not pity. And there was no justice for them. A man might work 12 hours a day for $2.50 or less. If he complained, there was always someone even hungrier waiting for his job.

As the twentieth century began, many Americans were very poor and only a few were very rich. Between one-third and one-half of the people barely had enough to eat, and the average worker earned $400 or $500 a year. At the same time industrialist Andrew Carnegie earned over $23 million in 1900 and paid no income tax because it did not yet exist.

Progressives like Jane Addams tried to bring some justice to the American way of life. They won the support of Presidents Theodore Roosevelt and Woodrow Wilson. As a result, corporations were more carefully regulated. A Pure Food and Drug Act was passed, and so was a federal income-tax law.

But the reformers had barely begun their work when World War I threatened. Jane Addams opposed war. She said it destroyed democracy and culture. She said the money that would be poured into tanks and munitions was needed to rebuild slums, set up schools and playgrounds, give mothers and children the care they needed.

She and other progressives worked hard to keep America at peace. When they failed, some of them abandoned the cause and supported the war. But Jane Addams remained a pacifist.

Earlier she had been one of the most honored women in America. Because of her views she became the object of hate and scorn. Wilson's stirring words and the propaganda of the CPI had worked too well. America became a land of one opinion, and that opinion was the President's.

Jane Addams never changed her mind about the war, but she did lower her voice. "We gradually ceased to state our position," she wrote, "as we became convinced that it served no practical purpose and, worse than that, often found that the immediate result was provocative."

**3**

# " I Am for Humanity "

*When I see suffering about me, I myself suffer, and so when I put forth my efforts to relieve others, I am simply helping myself. I do not consider that I have made any sacrifice whatever; no man does, unless he violates his conscience.*

Eugene Debs

Although Jane Addams and other progressives often wearied of the struggle to make themselves heard for peace, there was a fourth group of dissenters who were harder to silence. The members fell into the catch-all category of America's radicals.

The term *radical* covers a wide variety of people holding a wide variety of opinions. Radicals as often disagree with each other as with anyone else. But generally they are opposed to the existing economic or political system, or both.

Reformers believe the quality of life can be improved through education and legislation. Radicals believe the system is not worth saving. They want to change it completely. The question of how it should be changed and what should take its place has kept radicals writing and arguing for centuries.

What makes a man a radical? What made a man like Eugene Debs a radical? Most Americans believed radicals were long-haired, hot-eyed foreigners. But Eugene Debs was well dressed and clean shaven, and he came out of the heart of America.

Debs was born on November 5, 1855, in Terre Haute, Indiana. His father was a grocer.

During the Civil War, Terre Haute became an important railroad center. In the spring of 1870, Eugene Debs, 14 years old and already six feet tall, quit high school and went to work for the railroad.

His first job was cleaning grease from freight engines for 50 cents a day. When he was 16, he became a railroad fireman, shoveling coal into locomotive engines.

Debs's family worried about him because his work was so dangerous. The railroads were too concerned with making money to care about safe equipment. Accidents were common. When Debs was 19, a friend of his was run over by a locomotive. Debs's mother begged him to give up railroading, and he did. He became a clerk for a large grocery company in Terre Haute.

Debs worked on the railroads for only five years, but he learned a great deal. He learned about hard work and low pay. He saw men fired without notice, or maimed and killed by faulty equipment. He also traveled to other cities and saw jobless men and starving women and children.

When a union of locomotive firemen was organized in Terre Haute, Debs joined, even though he was no longer working for the railroad. But unions were weak then. They could do little about shorter hours or better pay. All that the firemen's union offered its members was cheap insurance. Considering the hazards of the job, they needed it.

Debs became active in the union but he was very conservative. In 1877 President Rutherford B. Hayes used federal troops to crush a major railroad strike. More than a hundred workers were killed and several hundred were wounded. Yet Debs criticized the strikers rather than the President. "A strike at the present time signifies anarchy and revolution," he said.

As the years passed, Debs became more and more popular in his home town. Running as a Democrat he served two terms as city clerk and one term in the Indiana state legislature. But when the legislature voted down several important reform bills he refused to run again.

Even while he was in office Debs continued to work for his own union and others as well. There were a lot of small, separate railroad unions representing the different crafts—engineers, firemen, brakemen, switchmen. Debs wanted a federation of all of these craft unions. This way they could stand together in a labor dispute. If necessary they could strike together. For Debs had come to believe that strikes were necessary. "The strike is the weapon of the oppressed," he said.

By 1889 Debs had organized a federation of railway unions. Although he was only in his thirties, he was called "the ablest labor speaker and writer in America." Some spoke of him as a possible candidate for President of the United States, for he was beginning to be an American legend. Everyone seemed to know that he would give the last dollar in his pocket to a widow or the coat on his back to a tramp.

The federation of railway unions soon fell apart because of internal quarrels. Then, in 1893, America suffered a major depression. Millions of men were without work. Those with jobs had to take sharp cuts in pay.

To help railroad workers during the depression, Debs organized the American Railway Union (ARU). It was an industrial union, open to anyone who worked for a railroad no matter what kind of job he held.

Railroad men rushed to join the ARU. Some were already members of craft unions. Others were unskilled workers who had never been offered union protection before. Debs traveled around the country signing up 200 to 400 members a day. "Labor can organize," he said. "This done, it can demand and command."

The ARU's first major battle was against the Great Northern Railroad, which was run by James J. Hill. Because of the depression, Hill had cut wages on the Great Northern down to about $1 a day. On April 13, 1894, his workers went out on strike.

Earlier railroad strikes had failed because there was no unity among the workers. But when Debs gave the order to support the strike, the members of the ARU obeyed. Hill's railroad was paralyzed, the union won almost everything it asked for, and Debs was a hero.

But labor was too weak and business too strong for any union victory to last. Within a month the ARU faced a more serious struggle with George M. Pullman.

*Eugene Debs was a hero to some, a villain to others. This critical cartoon portrays him as "King Debs" for tying up the country's railroads during the Pullman strike.*

Pullman was the man who made his fortune by inventing the railroad sleeping car. In a Chicago suburb he built a plant to manufacture Pullman cars. He also built a town around the plant for his workers. Every house, church, and even the library in Pullman, Illinois, was owned and run for profit by George Pullman.

During the depression of 1893, Pullman cut wages by half or more. But he didn't cut the rents in the houses where his workers lived. Thus one mechanic labored 10 hours a day for 12 days and earned seven cents. His actual wages had been $9.07 but the company had deducted $9 in advance for his rent.

During the winter of 1893 the workers in Pullman suffered and starved. By the spring of 1894, many of them had begun to join Debs's union. On May 11 those who had jobs went out on strike.

On Debs's orders, 125,000 railroad men supported the strikers by refusing to handle Pullman cars. Twenty railroads were tied up. It was at that time the largest strike in American history.

But instead of sympathizing with the strikers, many Americans turned against them. Men were hungry enough to take jobs as strikebreakers. Other union leaders were jealous enough of Debs to refuse to help him. Newspapers, which were owned by big businessmen, called the strike a war against the government. The *New York Times* said Debs drank too much.

On July 2 a Chicago court issued an order preventing Debs and other union leaders from taking part in the strike. If Debs obeyed the order the strike would fail. If he disobeyed he would go to jail. He decided to disobey.

Then on Independence Day, July 4, President Grover Cleveland sent troops to Chicago to break the strike. In the clashes that followed 30 persons were killed and 60 injured. More than 700 persons were arrested, including Eugene Debs.

The strike was broken but Debs was not. He was sent to jail for six months, which gave him a lot of time to think and read. He decided the worker did not have a chance in the capitalist system. Business controlled all sources of power, including government and the press.

Debs had been a Democrat all of his life. He had even campaigned for Grover Cleveland. But it was President Cleveland who had sent troops to Chicago. "I favor wiping out both old parties so they will never come into power again," said Debs.

In jail he became interested in socialism. This is the belief that all the major means of production and distribution—such as large industries, banks, and railroads—should be owned and operated by the people for the general welfare and not for private profit.

When Debs was released from jail in November 1895, he was more of a popular hero than ever. He had defied the railroads, the courts, and the government on behalf of the workers. Over 100,000 people came out to see and cheer him on his way home.

The following year Debs decided to give the Democratic Party one more chance because it ran a reformer, William Jennings Bryan, for President. Debs campaigned for Bryan, but conservative Republican William McKinley won.

Debs decided that all hope of progress through the major political parties was dead. "The issue is Socialism versus Capitalism," he wrote. "I am for Socialism because I am for humanity."

Debs became one of the founders of the Socialist Party of America. Every four years, from 1900 to 1912, he was the party's candidate for President of the United States. In 1912 he polled almost 900,000 votes. One admirer said, "That old man with the burning eyes actually believes there can be such a thing as the brotherhood of man. And that's not the funniest part of it. As long as he's around I believe it myself."

When World War I began in Europe, Debs supported neutrality. He believed the causes of the war were economic—the capitalist nations were simply fighting over markets and colonies.

In 1916 Debs was too ill and weary to run for President. But he saw America drawing closer to the war and spoke out against it. When war was declared the following April, some Socialists supported it, but Debs was not one of them.

"Let the capitalists do their own fighting and furnish their own corpses," he said, "and there will never be another war on the face of the earth."

## 4

# Down in the Gutter

*Hallelujah, I'm a bum,*
*Hallelujah, bum again,*
*Hallelujah, give us a handout—*
*To revive us again.*

American folk song

Eugene Debs was not the kind of man to swallow Wilson's preachings on how to build a better world at the point of a bayonet. The President would also have difficulties with another kind of radical. For the same conditions that made Debs a socialist bred America's wildest, most radical labor movement, the IWW. The initials stood for Industrial Workers of the World, but the members were most often called by the nickname of the Wobblies.

The IWW was organized in 1905 by a group of radical labor leaders and socialists, including Debs. They held different and often conflicting views, but they agreed on two things.

First, they opposed the capitalist system. "The working class and the employing class have nothing in common," said the preamble to the IWW constitution. "There can be no peace so long as hunger and want are found among millions of working people and the few, who make up the employing class, have all the good things of life."

Second, they believed that workers had to organize industrial unions. Ultimately they would form one big union of all workers regardless of race, sex, origin, craft, or skill.

But the beliefs that bound the IWW leaders together proved weaker than the issues that drove them apart. In 1908 the union divided into two factions. One was socialist. The other was called "anarcho-syndicalist."

Socialists, anarchists, and syndicalists all agree that the state is the tool of big business. The socialist answer is political action. Socialists want to take over the state on behalf of the workers.

The anarchist solution is to do away with the state entirely. Some anarchists are opposed to violence of any kind. Others are terrorists who want literally to destroy the state and its representatives with dynamite, bombs, and assassination.

Syndicalism was a movement that developed in France in the nineteenth century. Unions were to be organized not just for economic gains but to overthrow the capitalist system. A series of small strikes would lead to a general strike. This general strike would signal the universal uprising of the workers. They would seize control of all industries and rule in place of the state.

Anarcho-syndicalism, therefore, tied the wish to destroy the state to the economic struggle of the workers. Its weapons were industrial unionism and the general strike.

When the IWW split, the major portion fell into the hands of the anarcho-syndicalists. They were also called "the red-blooded working stiffs." Some of the angriest and most radical of these men advocated sabotage and theft to achieve their ends. They justified this by saying that all property is theft, that the bosses murdered them and stole their labor, and that human rights are more important than property rights.

But the IWW also functioned as a regular labor union. "We are going down in the gutter to get at the mass of the workers and bring them up to a decent plane of living," said William D. Haywood, the Wobbly leader.

For all its fiery talk, the IWW did what no other union would do. It deliberately sought out workers that other unions rejected—the unskilled, the blacks, the immigrants, the farm workers, the migratory laborers who wandered from place to place looking for a few days' pay.

The Wobblies organized across the country, from the textile mills of New England to the mining camps of Nevada and the timber ranges of the Northwest. They struck for higher pay and better working conditions, and sometimes won.

In time the Wobblies became champions of unpopular causes as well as unpopular people. One of these causes was the right to free speech.

Wobblies would go into a city or town and hold a

*"Join the One Big Union," said this IWW sticker. Business and government feared the Wobblies because one big union would challenge their economic and political power.*

series of street meetings. They usually opened with a few rousing choruses of "Hallelujah, I'm a Bum," an American folk song they adopted as their own. Then a speaker would try to recruit new members. He would attack labor conditions, especially for migrant workers. While he was at it, he might also attack religion, politics, and capitalism.

Local businessmen and patriots were infuriated by these rallies. They preferred not to hear what was wrong, especially if it was true. Wobblies were jailed, beaten, and tarred and feathered. Said one western sheriff, "When a Wobbly comes to town, I just knock him over the head with a nightstick and throw him in the river. When he comes up he beats it out of town."

The climax of the free-speech campaign came in the state of Washington. On November 5, 1916, some 300 Wobblies sailed from Seattle to Everett in two steamboats to hold a demonstration. When they tried to land, they were greeted by the gunfire of police and local vigilantes. Five Wobblies and two vigilantes were killed. More than 50 men were wounded.

When the Wobblies returned to Seattle, 74 of them were arrested for the murder of the two vigilantes. No one was arrested for murdering the five Wobblies. One of the Wobbly leaders was chosen to stand trial first. When he was acquitted, the other 73 men were released.

A few months after the Everett massacre America entered World War I. Wobbly leaders opposed all war in general and this one in particular. "What is this war all about?" asked Big Bill Haywood. The burly, one-eyed Wobbly chief had gone to work in the mines when he was eight years old. The only war he knew was the struggle to survive in his own country.

Some Wobblies went off to fight but most opposed the war. As one Wobbly put it, "If you were a bum without a blanket; if you had left your wife and kids when you went West for a job, and had never located them since; if your job never kept you long enough in a place to qualify you to vote; if you slept in a lousy, sour bunk-house, and ate food just as rotten as they could give you and get by with it . . . ; if every person who represented law and order and the nation beat you up, railroaded you to jail, and the good Christian people cheered and told them to go to it, how the hell do you expect a man to be patriotic?"

## 5

# Criticism a Crime

*Woe be to the man that seeks to stand in our way in this day of high resolution when every principle we hold dearest is to be vindicated and made secure.*

Woodrow Wilson

The Wobblies might well wonder what America could do for democracy abroad when she hadn't done much for it at home. But President Wilson was not the man to answer such a question. He didn't even want to hear it asked.

The same day Wilson called for a declaration of war, an espionage bill was introduced in Congress. Espionage is supposed to mean spying; every nation has laws to protect itself from spies. America already had a law to punish treason—but it applied to actual acts of betrayal. What Wilson was interested in was punishing not just acts but opinions as well.

The espionage bill was vigorously opposed by those who believed it would be used not just against spies but against anyone who disagreed with Wilson's war policy. One senator said, "We may well pause lest in our tenderness for democracy abroad we forget democracy at home."

But there was wide support for the bill, much of it drummed up by the press. The country was flooded by scare stories about "the enemy within." According to various sensational accounts German spies were running amok in America. They were planning to lead a black rebellion in the South. They were putting ground glass in food and bandages intended for the armed forces. They were poisoning wells and spreading tetanus and flu germs.

None of this was true, but it sold newspapers. It also created a climate of suspicion and hysteria.

Thus one congressman said to critics of the espionage bill, "Who is it to affect? The law-abiding citizen? Not at all. It is intended only to affect the criminal classes." And Wilson demanded passage of the bill as "absolutely necessary to the public safety."

The Espionage Act was passed by both houses of Congress in June and signed by the President on June

*Woodrow Wilson at his White House desk in 1917. Novelist John Dos Passos described the President as having been brought up "between the Bible and the dictionary."*

15, 1917. In one stroke, freedom of speech and freedom of the press were crippled in America.

Part of the act dealt with actual spying and the protection of military secrets. But the act also created several new offenses. Anyone who made "false reports or false statements with intent to interfere with" the war could be punished by up to 20 years in jail, a $10,000 fine, or both.

What was a false statement about the war? Any statement that disagreed with or contradicted official United States policy.

Loosely interpreted—and the Espionage Act of 1917 would be very loosely interpreted—any criticism of the war could be considered a crime. It was not just a question of an *act* of treason or spying. Any *opinion* contrary to the official view could be punished by 20 years in prison.

The act muffled not only freedom of speech but freedom of the press as well. Wartime censorship was supposed to be voluntary. Newspapers agreed not to print stories that would harm the war effort. But because of the new act, anyone who wrote or printed a story not approved by the Committee on Public Information could be accused of making "false statements" about the war. In addition, any publication that violated the Espionage Act could be barred from the mails.

Although some might think the Espionage Act went rather far toward destroying traditional American freedoms, Thomas Gregory, who was Attorney General at the time, did not think it went far enough. He asked Congress to stiffen a few of its provisions. In a burst of patriotism Congress went farther than Gregory asked and added a host of new offenses, with the same high penalties.

The amendment to the Espionage Act of June 1917 was signed by Wilson on May 16, 1918. It is often referred to as the Sedition Act. Sedition is difficult to define. It more or less covers acts or words that are dangerous enough to disturb the peace but not dangerous enough to be considered treason.

Under the Sedition Act of 1918 it became a crime

to say or write anything "disloyal . . . or abusive"
about the government, the Constitution, the flag, or
the army or navy uniform.

There was also a clause which forbade anyone to
urge "any curtailment of production . . . of any . . .
product . . . necessary or essential to the prosecution
of the war." This made it possible to label almost any
union activity in wartime a form of sedition.

Some critics said that under the new act the Democrats could outlaw the Republicans for criticizing
them. This interpretation was not as silly as it seemed.
Only once before had America passed a Sedition Act.
This was in 1798, which was also a period of tension
and hysteria. At that time it appeared that America
was headed for war with France.

In 1798 the President, John Adams, was a member
of the Federalist Party. He felt his opponents, the Republicans led by Thomas Jefferson, were too sym-
pathetic to the French. He also felt they were too
likely to win the next election.

As a result the Federalists passed a Sedition Act. It
became criminal to criticize the government, Congress, or the President. Under this act a Republican
congressman was tried, convicted, fined $1,000, and
sentenced to four months in prison. Republican journalists were also tried and punished.

But the Sedition Act of 1798 was used against only
two dozen persons. By the time it expired in 1801 it
had turned many Americans against the Federalists.
The party was voted out of office and eventually died
out.

The Espionage and Sedition Acts of 1917 and 1918

went much farther than the act of 1798. They would be applied more widely and more viciously. Never before in American history had the right of free speech been so threatened. Never before had an American government gone so far to silence its critics. Never before had it been so dangerous to dissent.

With these two acts of Congress, America's Reign of Terror began.

6

# The Spirit of Lawlessness

*Once lead this people into war, and they'll forget there ever was such a thing as tolerance. To fight you must be brutal and ruthless, and the spirit of ruthless brutality will enter into the very fiber of our national life, infecting Congress, the courts, the policeman on the beat, the man in the street. Conformity would be the only virtue . . . and every man who refused to conform would have to pay the penalty.*

Woodrow Wilson (April 1, 1917)

Civil liberties mean freedom. They especially mean freedom of thought and speech for persons who disagree and are sometimes disagreeable.

No one ever questions the right of free speech for someone who agrees with him. But that same right is often denied to those with another opinion. The majority does not like to be troubled by the voices of the minority. Civil liberties, therefore, are often unpopular because they protect minority opinions. They are most unpopular in time of war, because emotions run higher then.

Soon after the Constitution was adopted ten amendments were added. These are known as the Bill of Rights. Their purpose is to protect the people from the overwhelming power of the government.

The First Amendment says that "Congress shall make no law . . . abridging . . . freedom of speech or of the press." Yet in peace as well as war there may be times when words can be harmful. Supreme Court Justice Oliver Wendell Holmes once wrote, "The most stringent protection of free speech would not protect a man in falsely shouting fire in a theater and causing a panic."

Not even the Constitution gives a man the right to call for violence and murder. But what about the man who calls for an end to violence and murder? If free speech causes specific acts which are harmful it may be dangerous. But when free speech is condemned only because it is critical of those in power, democracy ceases to exist.

Yet most Americans in 1917 did not want to hear from their critics. They wanted them silenced by law and, if necessary, by force. It had been very simple for President Wilson to win support for the war because he controlled public opinion. But he not only sold the war, he oversold it.

Bombarded by propaganda about the German menace, Americans began howling for blood. But whose blood? The real enemy was three thousand miles away, across the ocean. Frenzied patriots had to find a substitute closer to home.

Since the press and politicians insisted spies were everywhere, hysterical Americans began to see them in the strangest places. Hunters in Michigan shot a new species of pigeon they said was German. The citizens of Kansas spotted mysterious planes in the night.

It was all part of the war fever. A man who was supposed to be a master spy from Germany turned out to be a plumber from Baltimore. Another man who was supposed to be signaling to an offshore German submarine was just changing a light bulb in his hotel room.

Instead of trying to cool the hysteria, the government poured on fuel. Attorney General Gregory urged every American to be a "volunteer detective" in the search for spies and subversives. He said "citizens should feel free to bring their suspicions and information" to the Justice Department. He welcomed complaints "of even the most informal and confidential nature." In short he asked every American to spy on every other American.

Even Gregory was startled by the response. One month after America entered the war the Justice Department was receiving 1,000 accusations of disloyalty a day. By the following year the daily total had swelled to 1,500.

Gregory admitted that most of the accusations were from "hysterical" men and women. He said they were "utterly worthless" and prompted by "malice and ill-will." But he didn't try to stop them. Throughout the war federal attorneys ran newspaper ads advising people it was their patriotic duty to report "disloyal acts."

Gregory made snooping not only respectable but official. Even before America entered the war, a businessman asked the Attorney General for permission to organize a group of volunteers to assist the Justice Department. Gregory agreed. He also got the consent of President Wilson and the entire cabinet.

The organization was called the American Protective League (APL). By the end of the war it boasted 350,000 members.

Members of the APL were authorized by the Justice Department to check the loyalty of friends, enemies, and strangers. They were also given the responsibility of checking the loyalty of government employees and men who wanted to be officers in the armed forces.

The APL conducted more than three million loyalty investigations. Not a single spy was uncovered but the lives and careers of many innocent persons were ruined. One man was accused of disloyalty because he was a member of the Democratic Party. Others were smeared because they belonged to unions.

Members of the APL used their special status to settle personal grudges, break strikes, and sell illegal whiskey. Some posed as federal agents and arrested people, though they had no authority to do so.

Attorney General Gregory knew of these abuses but he found the APL useful to maintain the Terror. He refused to disband the organization until after the

# Spies and Lies

*A CPI ad published in 1918. The man represents a German spy listening to a woman read aloud from a letter. "German agents are everywhere," warns the ad. "Report the man who spreads pessimistic stories, divulges—or seeks—confidential military information, cries for peace, or belittles our efforts to win the war."*

war ended. None of the members was ever prosecuted for his crimes.

The APL was the best organized of the witch-hunting clans that flourished during the war but it was not the only one. Many other Americans, privately or in groups, appointed themselves guardians of their neighbors' consciences. They decided who was disloyal and administered the punishment.

All across America there was a rash of vigilante crimes.

The Rev. William M. Hicks was tarred and feathered in Elk City, Oklahoma, because he was a pacifist.

Six farmers in Texas were horsewhipped because they would not contribute to the Red Cross.

The Rev. W. T. Sims, a black man, was lynched because he opposed the draft. Robert Prager, a white man, was lynched because someone thought he was a German sympathizer.

In America's first year at war, there were over 100 such incidents. When the Rev. Herbert Bigelow, a former pacifist who supported the war but didn't hate the Germans enough, was kidnapped by a masked band and beaten, there was a public outcry loud enough to rouse the President. Wilson finally spoke out against "the spirit of lawlessness."

But it continued. It continued because it was the spirit of the times. The mobs were acting out in blood what the Wilson administration was acting out in the courts. The vigilantes had their whips and tar pots. The government had its Espionage Act.

## 7

# Thoughts on Trial

*The President was against free speech in the height of the war. He said there could be no such thing.*

George Creel

When America entered the war, President Wilson had the army, the navy, the Justice Department, the various federal and police forces, and several perfectly good laws to deal with conspiracy or treason. But this was not enough for him.

First he tried to convert everyone to his view of the war. When he failed he blamed not himself but his critics.

He said repeatedly that the Espionage Act was not meant to shield him from criticism, but that is how it was most often used. The day after it was signed Postmaster General Albert S. Burleson issued an order. All local postmasters were to send him publications that violated the Espionage Act or that might "embarrass or hamper the Government in conducting the war." By Burleson's definition, embarrassing the government had become a federal crime.

Burleson's office was swamped with suspect newspapers, magazines, and leaflets. Within a month, issues of 15 major publications had been banned from the mails.

In several instances Burleson decided to destroy not just one issue but the entire magazine. Most publications could be sold and distributed profitably only through the mails. Therefore, the Postmaster General first found fault with a single issue and refused to mail it. Since that issue had to be skipped, Burleson then ruled the magazine was no longer being published regularly and was not entitled to the low postage rates for periodicals. In this way, by finding one article in one issue that offended him, Burleson could put publications permanently out of business.

No one ever knew where or when the Postmaster General might pounce. He refused to issue guidelines.

All he would reveal was that no publication could say "this Government got in the war wrong."

He and his aides seemed to work almost at whim.

An issue of one magazine was banned because it criticized Samuel Gompers, a conservative labor leader who supported the war.

An issue of another magazine was banned for suggesting that the war be paid for by taxes instead of loans.

Magazines were banned for criticizing the French or the British. One publication was banned for reprinting Thomas Jefferson's opinion that Ireland should be a republic.

Burleson never had to justify his acts because he was backed by the courts and the President. Throughout the war and long after it ended, he was the sole judge of which mailed publications Americans could or could not read.

The Espionage Act was used not just against periodicals, but against people as well. Since the act punished "false reports or false statements," anyone who expressed an opinion of the war that was contrary to the official view might be found to have made a "false statement." Only rarely did judges or juries consider that perhaps it was the government, not its critics, that was making the false statements.

Although the accused were entitled to trial by jury, this proved very little protection in a time of hysteria. One judge said later that jurors believed "the only verdict in a war case, which could show loyalty, was a verdict of guilty."

The most casual remarks were found to be not only false but made "with intent to interfere with" the war effort.

Rose Pastor Stokes wrote a letter to the editor of a newspaper. In it she said, "I am for the people, and the government is for the profiteers." Mrs. Stokes was sentenced to 10 years in prison.

D. H. Wallace, a former British soldier, said that "when a soldier went away he was a hero" and "when he came back . . . he was a bum." Wallace was sentenced to 20 years.

J. P. Doe wrote a chain letter in which he questioned the government's claim that Germany had promised to end submarine warfare. Doe was sentenced to 18 months.

Rev. Clarence H. Waldron handed out a pamphlet which said war was un-Christian. Rev. Waldron was sentenced to 15 years.

One of the unluckiest victims of the Espionage Act was Robert Goldstein, producer of a film called *The Spirit of '76*. The movie took a year and a half to make. Unfortunately for Goldstein it was released after America entered the war.

Since the film was about the American Revolution, the British were shown as villains. But this was 1917, not 1776, and the British were now allies. For his historical film on the birth of the nation, Goldstein was sentenced to 10 years in prison.

As though the federal law was not harsh enough, many states passed their own espionage acts. In Minnesota someone was convicted of discouraging women from knitting by saying, "No soldier ever sees these socks."

As a result of federal, state, and private persecution, a blanket of fear and silence fell over the country. Most Americans accepted the situation; only a few dared to fight back. In October 1917, the National Civil Liberties Bureau (NCLB) was organized to defend the freedoms the government is supposed to preserve, not suppress.

But the leaders of the NCLB found that many liberals, both as individuals and in groups, shied away from them. Even gentle Jane Addams refused to help. "I am obliged to walk very softly in regard to all things suspect," she wrote.

The NCLB was highly suspect. To the government, the fight for civil liberties was just another form of sedition. The Wilson administration did all it could to harass the NCLB. NCLB publications were banned from the mails, and the Justice Department stopped just short of persecuting the organization out of existence.

Some people hoped the Supreme Court might bring the nation back to sanity when it ruled on the Espionage Act. America had faced far greater danger during the Civil War. Yet the Supreme Court had declared that the Constitution applied "equally in war and in peace . . . at all times, and under all circumstances."

However, it usually takes a long time for a case to come before the Supreme Court. The Civil War was over when this decision was handed down. In the same way, World War I was over when the Supreme Court finally ruled on the Espionage Act in 1919.

The court's decisions gave no comfort to those who opposed the Espionage Act. The act was found to be constitutional. The first decision was *Schenck v. United States.* This was one of the few prosecutions in which the defendants had actually attempted to interfere with the war effort. They had urged young men to resist the draft.

The Supreme Court unanimously affirmed their guilt. In writing the decision Justice Holmes offered what would become an important rule for balancing individual rights against the public interest.

"The question in every case," he wrote, "is whether the words used are used in such circumstances and are of such a nature as to create a clear and present danger . . . that Congress has a right to prevent." Thus free speech might be curbed if it presented a "clear and present danger" to the nation's security.

But the court continued to uphold the Espionage and Sedition Acts even when there was no clear and present danger. In the case of *Abrams v. United States,* some socialists had written and distributed a leaflet. It attacked Wilson for sending American troops to Russia in the summer of 1918 to help try to crush the Russian Revolution.

The defendants were found guilty of violating the Sedition Act. Three of them were sentenced to 20 years. Two others got shorter terms.

The majority of the Supreme Court affirmed the convictions. Holmes and Justice Louis Brandeis dissented. Holmes could find no clear and present danger. The pamphlets had nothing to do with the war with Germany. The Espionage and Sedition Acts were to apply only in wartime, and America had not declared war on Russia.

Holmes found the Abrams case "persecution for the expression of opinions." Then he warned, "I think that we should be eternally vigilant against attempts to check the expression of opinions that we loathe."

But Holmes was in the minority both on the court and in the country. Altogether there were 1,956 prosecutions under the federal Espionage and Sedition Acts. As a result 877 persons were found guilty.

Not one of them was a German spy.

## 8

# End of a Union

*I love my flag, I do, I do,*
*Which floats upon the breeze.*
*I also love my arms and legs,*
*And neck and nose and knees.*
*One little shell might spoil them all*
*Or give them such a twist*
*They would be of no use to me;*
*I guess I won't enlist.*

IWW poem

When America thrashed about for victims during the war hysteria, her wrath did not just fall on individual sinners. Two groups took most of the blows. During a period when conformity was the only virtue, they continued to be different. They were the IWW and the Socialists.

All unions suffered to some extent during the war. For most of its history, America had been a rural nation. Even though more Americans now worked in factories than on farms, many people considered unions foreign to the original American ideal of rugged individualism. Americans tended to be anti-union before the war; while it raged a strike seemed nothing less than treason.

Most union men and their leaders supported the war. But they also supported their rights. They struck in wartime not because they were pro-German but because they had families to feed.

In the first six months of the war, unions that were affiliated with the conservative American Federation of Labor (AFL) took part in 518 strikes. In that same period the IWW led only three strikes, yet popular anger fell on the Wobblies.

The Wobblies were considered subversive even before the war began. They criticized the government and big business too much. They cared too much about the poor, the immigrant, the black, all of whom more comfortable Americans wanted to forget. Most of all, they talked too much about anarchy and violence. Much of it was just talk; AFL unions committed more industrial sabotage than the IWW. But people still feared the Wobblies.

When America went to war some Wobblies enlisted in the armed forces. Their leaders generally opposed the war but couldn't agree on what to do about it. A small group wanted to defy the draft and call a general strike. But the majority opposed any anti-war activity. It would take time and energy from the main task of organizing the workers. Big Bill Haywood said, "The world war is of small importance compared to the great class war."

Besides, Wobbly leaders knew they had to be careful. Anti-war activity on their part would give the government an excuse to destroy the union.

So the IWW went about its business of fighting for better working conditions, especially in the mining and timber regions of the West. But the owners of the mines and forests wanted to be rid of the Wobblies. In wartime it was easy to charge that the union was really trying to help not the workers but the Germans.

This cry was quickly picked up by the press and the politicians, both of whom were anxious to serve big business. It was fresh meat to the spy-chasers who were colliding with each other in their eagerness to find new victims.

The persecution of the Wobblies, like the other wartime persecutions, began with brute force. Wobblies were beaten and lynched by vigilante bands who were usually prodded or paid by business interests.

In Arizona the copper owners, whose profits were soaring because of war orders, cut wages. The IWW led a strike in protest.

In July 1917, a group of vigilantes in the town of Bisbee seized 1,200 Wobblies, strikers, and sympathizers. They forced them aboard a 27-car cattle train and sent them under armed guard to New Mexico. The men were left in the desert for 36 hours without food or water. Then they were beaten, sent to prison, and held without charges. They were released three months later.

A presidential commission investigated the Arizona copper strike and the Bisbee outrage. The commission found that many of the men who were kidnapped supported the war and some were veterans. It concluded that the strike had nothing to do with the war but was a legitimate attempt to win better working conditions.

Labor troubles in the copper mines of Butte, Montana, were also settled by the mob. Before dawn on August 1, 1917, an IWW organizer named Frank Little was dragged from his hotel room by six masked men. After beating Little, the lynchers tied him to the rear fender of a car and dragged him out of town along a dirt road. Then they hanged him.

Brute force to break the IWW was also supplied by the government. The army was used to crush lumber and copper strikes in the summer of 1917. Troops dispersed strikers, raided IWW halls, and threw members in jail without warrants or charges.

But the government would not settle for simple strikebreaking. President Wilson disliked the IWW. He said it was "worthy of being suppressed," and he had the power to see that this was done.

On September 5, 1917, federal agents raided 48 IWW offices around the country. They arrested everyone they could find and seized five tons of union literature and letters.

After the first swoop agents continued to raid Wobbly halls. They arrested thousands of Wobblies, held them for a few days, and then released them. Their purpose was to frighten the men into quitting the

*Some of the 1,200 Wobblies and other strikers in the custody of the armed vigilantes of Bisbee, Arizona.*

union. The government also wanted to leave them no
union to belong to.

On April 1, 1918, some 100 IWW leaders and
members, both white and black, were put on trial in
Chicago. They were charged with violating the Espionage Act, as well as several other statutes. But they
were tried not so much for what they did as for what
they thought. The prosecutor said plainly, "It is the
IWW which is on trial here."

When the trial finally ended in mid-August, the ju-

rors had four and one-half months of testimony to consider. They also had to weigh specific charges against 100 different defendants. Yet it took less than one hour to find everyone guilty.

Big Bill Haywood and 14 other important Wobblies were sentenced to 20 years in prison. The rest got up to 10 years. In addition the men were fined a total of more than $2,500,000.

The Chicago trial was followed by trials of smaller groups of Wobblies in other parts of the country. In this way the leaders of the IWW were jailed and the union treasury was emptied.

Using the war as an excuse, the government succeeded in effectively destroying the union.

# 9

# A Free Soul in Jail

*I abhor war. . . . When I think of a cold, glittering steel bayonet being plunged into the . . . quivering flesh of a human being, I recoil with horror.*

Eugene Debs

World War I divided the Socialists even more than it did the IWW. Some left the Socialist Party and were reborn as hawks. Those who chose to oppose the war faced the penalties of the Espionage Act and the wrath of the vigilantes.

Eugene Debs watched the destruction of his cause

and his friends with mounting dismay. At first he was not certain what he should do. Then he decided he had to speak out, though he knew what would happen. "Of course, I'll take about two jumps and they'll nail me," he said, "but that's all right."

On June 16, 1918, Debs spoke in Canton, Ohio, at the state convention of the Socialist Party. "It is extremely dangerous," he told his audience, "to exercise the constitutional right of free speech in a country fighting to make democracy safe in the world."

Then he added, "I would a thousand times rather be a free soul in jail than to be a . . . coward in the streets."

Debs spoke in a park to a crowd of about 1,200 persons. Among them were federal agents and volunteers from the American Protective League. A 20-year-old stenographer had been hired by the Justice Department to record the speech. But his shorthand was bad and he got only parts of it.

Debs spent most of his speech attacking the capitalist system rather than the war. But he also said, "The master class has always declared the wars; the subject class has always fought the battles. The master class has had all to gain and nothing to lose, while the subject class has had nothing to gain and all to lose—especially their lives."

Two weeks later Debs was arrested for violating the Espionage Act. "I had a hunch that speech was likely to settle the matter," he said cheerfully.

But others were not so cheerful about it. They were shocked.

Even while the government was violating the liberties of thousands of Americans, their countrymen looked the other way. Most Americans either were unconcerned about the wartime persecutions or cheered them on. They thought of pacifists and radicals as troublemakers. They saw the Wobblies as hoboes. They didn't think such people had any rights. What they didn't realize was that when no one protects the rights of the minority, the majority may be next.

Debs led an unpopular minority but he was not an unpopular man. He had won six percent of the vote when he ran for President in 1912. He was neither a foreigner nor a terrorist. He not only was a native American but looked and acted like one. He carried grocery bags for old ladies and gave candy to children. It was hard to think of him as a traitor.

Debs went on trial on September 9, 1918, in Cleveland, Ohio. He denied nothing the government said about him. All he asked for was permission to speak to the jury.

For nearly two hours he told the jurors how he felt about socialism, capitalism, and war. He said he had a right to oppose a war he did not believe in and that some of the country's greatest statesmen, including Abraham Lincoln, had opposed America's war with Mexico.

He concluded with the words, "I do not know, I cannot tell, what your verdict may be; nor does it matter much, so far as I am concerned. . . . I am not on trial here. . . . American institutions are on trial

*Eugene Debs making a speech before the war. This "tall shamblefooted man," said Dos Passos, "had a sort of gusty rhetoric that set on fire the . . . workers." He "made them want the world he wanted . . . where everybody would split even."*

here before a court of American citizens. The future will tell."

The jury found Debs guilty. Before he was sentenced on September 14 he made another statement. "Your Honor," he said to the judge, "years ago I recognized my kinship with all living things, and I made up my mind that I was not one bit better than the meanest of the earth.

"I said then, I say now, that while there is a lower class, I am in it; while there is a criminal element, I am of it; while there is a soul in prison, I am not free."

The judge sentenced the 63-year-old Socialist to 10 years. The Supreme Court later upheld the verdict.

Eugene Debs went to prison on April 13, 1919. It happened to be Palm Sunday. It also happened that by then the war Debs was accused of interfering with had been over for five months.

## 10

# A New Scapegoat

*My Fellow Countrymen: The armistice was signed this morning. Everything for which America fought has been accomplished. It will now be our fortunate duty to assist by example, by sober, friendly counsel, and by material aid in the establishment of just democracy throughout the world.*

Woodrow Wilson

World War I ended on November 11, 1918. America and the Allies had won. Believing he had made the world safe for democracy, President Wilson was now anxious to establish it everywhere, using his own country as an example. But what kind of example?

According to the National Civil Liberties Bureau, America had 1,472 political prisoners either in jail or awaiting trial. As soon as peace came, Wilson was asked to free these people. Words believed to be harmful in war could now be forgiven.

This was particularly true since Wilson seemed to

be agreeing with some of his critics. He said in one speech, "The real reason that the war that we have just finished took place was that Germany was afraid her commercial rivals were going to get the better of her. . . . This war . . . was a commercial and industrial war. It was not a political war."

For saying much the same thing Debs and many others were behind bars. But when Wilson was asked to issue a general pardon he refused. "I do not think the men you refer to are in any proper sense political prisoners," he said. "They have in fact violated criminal statutes of the United States."

The President also refused to release the aged, ailing Eugene Debs. Wilson told his secretary, Joseph Tumulty, "This man was a traitor to his country and he will never be pardoned during my administration."

When Debs heard this he said of the President, "It is he, not I, who needs a pardon."

Persecution for unpopular ideas did not decrease when the war ended; it multiplied. During the war the government had planted the seeds of conformity and intolerance. In due time these seeds sprouted forth to poison the peace.

Peace was unsettling in many ways. To begin with, it soon became plain that this war had been no different from other wars after all. When discussions of peace terms began, it was clear that whatever Wilson's motives had been his allies had fought for the usual reasons of seizing what they could from their enemies.

Then American soldiers began returning from

France to tell their stories without the cover of government censorship. They revealed that the war had been bloody, dirty, and senseless. Feeling betrayed and bitter, many Americans blamed their European allies. They began to turn against both foreign entanglements and foreigners.

The returning veterans presented another problem. There were no jobs for them.

For four years America had been fattening on war orders. Now businesses that made war supplies collapsed. Some nine million workers had to find new jobs. So did four million veterans.

Even those lucky enough to be working suffered, for the war was followed by a wild inflation. Prices soared. The cost of living doubled between 1914 and 1919.

Disillusion, unemployment, and inflation made America tense and angry. During the war Americans had been trained to the scapegoat theory. If something is wrong, don't try to solve it, but find someone to blame. If the Wobblies say that children are starving and workers are underpaid, don't feed the children or raise the pay; jail the Wobblies.

While the war was on, anything that went wrong was blamed on Germans abroad and radicals at home. With the war over, a new foreign scapegoat had to be found. Events in Russia provided one—the Bolshevik.

The word *Bolshevik* has no political meaning. It comes from the Russian word for majority. But it was

*The propaganda of panic. This cartoonist showed the Bolsheviks and the Wobblies working hand-in-hand as the Devil's disciples.*

the name used by a faction of Russian Communists led by Lenin.

In November 1917, the Bolsheviks had seized power in Russia. They had difficulty establishing Communist rule there and civil war soon erupted. But this did not stop them from preaching revolution elsewhere. Lenin called upon the workers of the world to overthrow the ruling classes.

For a brief time Communists took power in Bavaria and Hungary. Almost everywhere, the ruling classes panicked. Perhaps this was indeed the beginning of the world revolution.

As World War I drew to a close, the anti-German crusade turned into an anti-Bolshevik crusade. At different times between 1918 and 1921, English,

French, Czech, German, Polish, Japanese, Italian, and American troops fought on Russian soil either to seize territory or to stop the revolution.

In the Bolsheviks, America now had a new foreign scapegoat. The domestic scapegoat remained the radical. But the end of hostilities made persecuting radicals more difficult because the Espionage and Sedition Acts applied only in wartime.

Because the war did not officially end until peace treaties were signed in the summer of 1921, the government continued to pretend it was still in effect. Men were still prosecuted for saying the wrong things. The Postmaster General continued to ban publications he didn't like.

But the Wilson administration knew it could not continue this fiction forever. Someday the war had to end, even officially. Wilson asked Congress to pass a peacetime sedition law. Until then the government would attack radical opinion through another route.

## 11

# The Unwanted Alien

*Nothing will save the life of this free Republic if these foreign leeches are not cut and cast out.*

Mrs. George T. Guernsey, president-general,
Daughters of the American Revolution

The route the government chose was not a new one. It was almost as old as American history.

In 1798, when America feared a war with France, Congress passed not only a Sedition Act but several Alien Acts as well.

The Act Respecting Alien Enemies gave the government the power to arrest and deport citizens of any country with which America was at war. During World War I, Wilson used this old law of 1798 to put more than 6,000 German aliens into prison camps.

The Act Concerning Aliens, also passed in 1798, gave the President the power to expel any alien he considered to be dangerous. The President did not have to give his reasons and the alien had no defense. This act expired within two years without ever being used. But the pattern had been set. In times of crisis, America had a ready scapegoat—the alien.

America is a nation of immigrants. No one is native to the land except the Indians. But it is not uncommon for a group of immigrants already ashore to regard the next boatload as intruders.

Until late in the nineteenth century, most immigrants came from western Europe—England, Germany, and Scandinavia. Then promise of a better life across the seas reached the people of southern and eastern Europe. By the 1880s, a fresh wave of immigration had begun. Most of the newcomers were Slavs, Italians, and Jews.

The older immigrant groups viewed the newer ones with distaste and hostility. They saw them as "beaten men from beaten races."

The new migration came at a time of great unrest in America. There were major depressions, strikes, and bombings. Rather than blame the industrial and economic conditions that were at fault, many people blamed the aliens who were among those fighting for justice. "There is no such thing as an American anarchist," wrote one angry journalist.

Repeated attempts were made to pass laws to rid the country of what were called "dangerous aliens," but none succeeded. Then, in September 1901, a man named Leon Czolgosz assassinated President William McKinley. Czolgosz was born in America and he was insane. But his name sounded foreign and he claimed he was an anarchist.

As a result of the assassination there was such anger against foreign agitators that Congress passed the Immigration Act of 1903. Immigrants who were anarchists, or members of any organization that advocated anarchy, could no longer enter the country. If one slipped by he could be deported within three years after his arrival.

For the first time in American history immigrants were barred for holding certain *beliefs* no matter how peacefully they might *behave*.

Three years later a new Naturalization Act was passed. To become a citizen an alien had to prove he was "attached to [the] principles of the Constitution." Naturalization officials often mistook opposition to capitalism for opposition to the Constitution. As a result they denied citizenship to socialists or members of the IWW.

The IWW was one of the prime targets of the next major change in the immigration laws. Before Amer-

*An anti-immigrant cartoon of the period. Mother Europe sweeps her "undesirable" citizens onto America's shores, as she complains, "My! How the dirt accumulates."*

ica entered World War I, and the IWW was destroyed by the Espionage Act, business and government had tried to find other ways of wiping it out. One was through immigration laws.

It was mistakenly believed that most Wobblies were aliens. Since it was so hard to find Wobblies guilty of specific crimes it seemed simpler just to deport them.

A new Immigration Act was passed in February 1917. Aliens could now be excluded or deported if they advocated or taught "the unlawful destruction of property," as some Wobblies did.

The act of 1917, which ran to many pages, was supposed to clarify immigration policy, but instead made it more confusing.

The act listed all the types of radical immigrants who could not enter the country. These included persons who believed in—or belonged to organizations that believed in—anarchy, violent overthrow of the government, assassination, and unlawful destruction of property. If such persons entered they could be deported within five years.

On the other hand, immigrants who became radicals *after* coming to America, and advocated any of the forbidden activities, could be deported at any time.

During the war, western business interests wanted the Immigration Act used to deport Wobbly leaders. But there were two loopholes in the law. First, there was the five-year time limit on deporting those who had entered as radicals. Second, those who became radicals after coming to America could be deported for *advocating* or *teaching* certain acts, but not for simply *believing* in them. Some proof of individual guilt was required.

Congress decided to seal off all escape hatches. On October 16, 1918, another immigration act became law. It is usually called the Deportation Act because that was its purpose.

There was no longer a time limit for anyone. Any unwanted alien could be deported at any time. Belief in certain ideas or membership in certain organizations was sufficient cause for deportation. Proof of individual guilt was no longer necessary.

The law was passed with the IWW in mind. But it would be used much more widely than that. As America sank deeper and deeper into her postwar crisis, many Americans became convinced there was only one possible cure. The country would survive only if alien radicals were sent back where they came from.

*12*

# Strikes and Bombs

*Whenever there is trouble of any sort in America there are voices shouting, "Bolshevism."*

SYRACUSE POST-STANDARD (July 29, 1919)

America might not have sought a scapegoat if 1919 had not been such a frightening year.

First there were the strikes.

Since prices were doubling, workers demanded more pay. When they were refused, they struck. In that one year there were some 3,600 strikes involving more than four million workers.

Four of these strikes particularly panicked the nation.

In January, 35,000 men who worked in the shipyards of Seattle, Washington, struck for higher wages and shorter hours. To support them other labor leaders in Seattle called a general strike. Until now only the employers had power. The unions, which represented many different kinds of workers, wanted to prove that if they stuck together they would have power too.

On February 6, 60,000 workers went on strike in Seattle. The city was paralyzed. The strikers made certain that people had food and fuel and that the garbage was collected. But all other services ceased.

There was no violence and no one was arrested. Yet to many Americans this seemed to be not just a strike but the beginning of the dreaded Bolshevik revolution. The citizens of Seattle armed themselves, and the fear flared far beyond the city, largely fanned by the press.

When the war ended American newspapers had found themselves with little to write about. They soon discovered that Bolshevik scare stories sold just as well as German scare stories. They reported the Seattle strike with such screaming headlines as: REDS DIRECTING SEATTLE STRIKE TO TEST CHANCE FOR REVOLUTION.

Politicians also exploited the hysteria. Mayor Ole Hanson of Seattle had ambitions for higher office. He announced, "The anarchists in this community shall not rule its affairs," and called in federal troops.

Astonished by the reaction to the strike, the Seattle labor leaders called it off on the fifth day. They had wanted neither Bolshevism nor anarchy, just a living wage. But Mayor Hanson announced, "The rebellion is quelled." A few months later he resigned to tour the country to lecture on the perils of Bolshevism.

The other three critical strikes that year took place in the fall. By then it was clear that any demand for better working conditions could be silenced with a Red smear. "Unionism is nothing less than Bolshevism" was the new employer creed.

In September, most of the police force in Boston, Massachusetts, went on strike. The men wanted to be affiliated with the conservative American Federation of Labor. No one could be less Red than the Boston police, but the strike was immediately labeled a "skirmish with Bolshevism."

Although the striking policemen voted to return to work after a few days, every one of them was fired.

That same month some 365,000 steel workers struck. Many of them worked 12 hours a day, seven days a week, for an average of $28 weekly. But steel executives denounced the strike as "un-American." They ran newspaper ads calling on the steel workers to GO BACK TO WORK AND STAND BY AMERICA—as though hunger were a new form of patriotism. The *Wall Street Journal* announced that the steel companies were "fighting the battle of the American Constitution."

When company guards broke up picket lines, fired on the strikers, and brought in strikebreakers, there were riots. These were blamed on the Bolsheviks. Public opinion stood so solidly behind the steel companies that the strikers were forced to go back to work. The strike had gained them nothing and cost 20 lives.

As the steel strike was dying, almost 400,000 coal

miners walked off their jobs seeking better wages and working conditions. Their leader, John L. Lewis, was bitterly anti-Communist. But the mine owners declared the strike was ordered by Lenin himself, and the government got a court order that killed it. Once again employers had been able to smother legitimate union activity with Red smoke.

Besides the strikes in 1919 there were also the bombs.

With everyone seeking signs and omens of the Bol-

*Strikes were often broken by police, soldiers, or company thugs. Here, a policeman beats a demonstrator during a strike in Philadelphia in 1919.*

shevik revolution, there were several bomb scares early in the year. But nothing actually happened until April 28.

On that day a homemade bomb arrived at the office of Mayor Hanson of Seattle. It was discovered before it exploded. The following day a similar bomb was delivered to the home of a former Georgia senator. When his maid opened the package it blew off her hands.

Within the next few days 34 more bombs were discovered in the mails and intercepted before anyone else was hurt. They had been addressed to important judges, cabinet members, senators, and businessmen. With only a few exceptions, all were likely targets of radical wrath.

All the bombs were mailed just before May Day, the labor and radical holiday. Many people assumed that radical terrorists had plotted a mass May Day execution. Without any evidence the *New York Times* blamed the "Bolsheviki, anarchists and IWW's." Calmer newspapers suggested that while one or two crazed terrorists might have been involved there was no need to surrender to panic.

Federal agents and local police spent months investigating the 36 bombs. No one was ever arrested and no evidence was found to link the bombs to any radical movement. Radical leaders claimed the bombs had been planted by police or federal agents to justify arrests and persecutions.

The bomb scare of May was followed by a second round in June. On the night of June 2, eight bombs exploded in eight different cities. Two persons were killed and several buildings were shattered.

In Washington, D.C., a bomb damaged the home of the new Attorney General, A. Mitchell Palmer. Palmer was unhurt, but parts of the body of the man who had probably set off the bomb were found in the debris. Copies of an anarchist pamphlet were scattered about the neighborhood.

Police identified the man as an alien from Philadelphia. As before, everyone accused the radicals. The radicals said they had been framed. The press called for "a few free treatments in the electric chair."

But there was no one to execute. All the federal agents and all the policemen couldn't put a case together again. Radical terrorists may have been guilty, but no one was able to prove it. No links were found to the radical movement and no one was arrested.

*13*

# The New Negro

*The . . . riots are bright spots in the new Negro's attitude toward American lawlessness and anarchy.*

THE MESSENGER

In addition to the strikes and bombings, 1919 was also a year of riots. Several of them occurred during the steel strike. Company agents were ordered to "stir up as much bad feeling as you possibly can" between different nationalities and between whites and blacks. If the workers could be made to fight each other, instead of the employers, the strike would collapse.

Elsewhere there were anti-radical riots, especially on May 1. The worst were in Boston, New York, and Cleveland. In each of these cities mobs including police and servicemen broke up radical parades and meetings. They also smashed Socialist Party offices.

It was people who demanded law and order who did the rioting—but the police arrested only radicals. Newspapers criticized the victims rather than the attackers. They said the May Day parades were merely dress rehearsals for the revolution.

The most serious riots of the year, however, were race riots. There were some 25 of them all the way from Washington, D.C., to Longview, Texas. They meant that blacks would no longer accept the role of victim to the white mob. "When the mob moves, we propose to meet it with bricks and clubs and guns," said black leader W. E. B. Du Bois.

The change in attitude was largely a result of the war. Both black and white troops were sent abroad to fight for democracy. Even though the blacks fought in segregated units, they were treated better than they ever had been before. Some became officers. Others saw how much less discrimination there was in Europe than in America.

Having helped make the world safe for democracy abroad, the black soldier began to wonder about democracy at home. Most blacks were forced to live in a segregated society where everything was not only separate but inferior.

The white man not only determined the black man's place but expected him to accept it. If the black strayed there was always a lynch mob waiting.

On September 28, 1919, in Omaha, Nebraska, a white mob decided to lynch a black man named William Brown. Brown was in jail in the county courthouse.

When the mob demanded its victim the mayor of Omaha, Edward P. Smith, refused to give him up. The mob seized Mayor Smith and tried to hang him from a trolley pole. Police cut the rope and just managed to save the mayor's life.

After failing to lynch their mayor the good citizens of Omaha began to stone the courthouse. They also fired at police who were defending the building.

When this seemed to be getting nowhere, some men started a fire on the first floor of the courthouse. The other prisoners, fearful of being roasted alive, surrendered Brown. He was shot and hanged at once.

Blacks who had fought for democracy refused to accept this kind of justice any longer. "Unless the white American behaves," warned a black editor, "he will find that in teaching our boys to fight for him he was starting something that he will not be able to stop."

Of all the race riots that year, the worst was in Chicago. It began at a beach on the steamy Sunday afternoon of July 27.

Five black teenagers were playing and swimming around a homemade log raft in the waters of Lake Michigan. As they floated by a breakwater, a white man began to fling rocks at them. The boys thought it was a game. They did not know that a riot had broken out nearby because blacks had tried to use a beach whites considered their own.

Whether the white man was throwing the rocks in fun or anger is not known. But the boys were not afraid. The man was at least 75 feet away. When they saw a rock coming they simply ducked under the water.

Suddenly it was no longer a game. One of the boys clinging to the side of the raft was Eugene Williams. For an instant Williams turned his head to speak to one of his friends. He never saw the rock which came hurtling through the air and crashed into his forehead.

Williams sank into water about 15 feet deep. The other four boys could see blood rising to the surface. They were terrified and, besides, none of them could swim very well. One of the boys tried to save Williams but failed. The four boys then quickly swam to shore and found a lifeguard. But it was too late. Eugene Williams had drowned.

The boys found a black policeman and took him to the beach where they pointed out the man they thought had thrown the rocks. But a white policeman who was on duty there refused to arrest the man. He also refused to let the black policeman arrest him. Instead, the white policeman arrested a black for some minor offense.

Word of the incident raced around the city. Exaggeration made the details even uglier than they were. Blacks and whites stormed to the beach and began flinging rocks and bricks at each other.

When police tried to take away the black man who had been arrested, another black named James Crawford fired and wounded a policeman. A black policeman returned the fire and killed Crawford.

The rioting and gunfire at the beach were only the

*The 1919 Chicago race riot left a trail of blood and wreckage across the city. Most Americans preferred to believe radicalism rather than racism was responsible.*

beginning. For five days blacks and whites shot, stabbed, and beat each other in the streets of Chicago. When the riot was over, 23 blacks and 15 whites were dead. Over 500 persons were injured.

Americans reacted sharply to the race riots in Chicago and elsewhere. Black publications were proud of what they called "the new Negro." The *Messenger*

wrote that the riots "represent the new Negro uphold-
ing the dignity of the law against both the white
hoodlums and the Government, the latter of whom
should have seen that the law was upheld."

But the *New York Times* complained that the war
had ruined the blacks. "The Negroes, before the great
war, were well behaved," it noted.

Very few whites understood that blacks were rioting because they were abused and angry. In the year
of the Red haze, the obvious explanation was that the
otherwise contented blacks had been stirred up by
evil outsiders. Thus the *Times* announced, "Bolshevist
agitation has been extended among the Negroes."

It was much easier to accept this reasoning than to
try to remake American society. The Justice Department investigated the riots and black radicalism. The
final report was prepared by the young chief of the
department's new anti-radical division, J. Edgar Hoover.

The Hoover report suggested that the black fight
for equality was unpatriotic, un-American, and sedi-
tious. It declared that some black leaders were opposed "to the Government and to the established rule
of law and order."

Hoover, his superiors at the Justice Department,
and most Americans believed that radicalism rather
than racism was the cause of the unrest. But black
leaders knew better. One group of them wrote: "Un-
just conditions . . . are the true Bolshevik propaganda. . . . Allay the discontent of the Negro population by according justice to it."

# 14

# 100% Americanism

*When a nation is filled with strife, then do patriots flourish.*

Lao-tzu, Chinese philosopher

Americans were in a lynching mood in 1919 not just in Omaha or Chicago but in all parts of the country. With every new disaster, press and politicians cried, "Bolshevik!" If the Bolsheviks were poisoning the American system the only cure was to find and destroy them.

During the war Americans had looked for German spies. Since there were scarcely any around, a great many innocent people suffered instead.

During the Red Scare of 1919 everyone went hunting Bolsheviks. Since there were very few of them either, a great many innocent people suffered in their place.

Brave as witch hunters are, they usually prefer to work in packs. A number of super-patriotic societies were formed to enforce what was called "100% Americanism." No one could say precisely what a 100% American was, but it helped to be white, Protestant, and American-born. Catholics, Jews, aliens, and blacks were suspect. So were union men and liberals. Anyone who was somehow different was not 100% American. Anyone who wanted change was not 100% American.

Among the patriotic societies were the National

Association of Manufacturers (NAM) and other employer groups. Their object was to equate loyalty to
America with loyalty to America's economic system.
Their immediate aim was to use the Red Scare to destroy the union movement.

Businessmen also financed many smaller but
equally effective super-patriotic organizations. These
groups proclaimed that Bolshevism was running wild
in the schools, press, church, and labor movement.
They told Americans which magazines to read and
which to burn. In many places they had textbooks
banned and teachers fired because of their views.

The businessmen provided the bankroll and the pa-
triotic societies provided the noise and the pressure.
But there was a third group that provided the muscle.
This was the American Legion.

The Legion was founded in May 1919 by veterans
of World War I. By the end of the year it had more
than one million members.

Legionnaires used fists, whips, and tar to foster
their view of 100% Americanism. It became common
to say, "Leave the Reds to the Legion."

Centralia, Washington, was one place where the
Reds were left to the Legion. In Centralia, a small
remnant of the IWW still survived and was battling
the lumber owners. When the owners decided to get
rid of the Wobblies they chose the Legion as their in-
strument.

First, Legionnaires made a trip to the Wobbly hall
in Centralia, beating, looting, and smashing. But the
Wobblies suspected the real clash would come on

November 11, the first anniversary of Armistice Day.

The Legionnaires had scheduled a parade whose route took them past the IWW hall. Many of the marchers were armed. So were the Wobblies, who waited in the hall and at strategic locations outside.

The paraders marched by once without incident. Then they decided to retrace their steps. This time the Legionnaires rushed the hall.

One of the Wobbly leaders was a lumberjack named Wesley Everest. Everest, who had fought in World War I, wore his army uniform that day. He told the other Wobblies, "I fought for democracy in France and I'm going to fight for it here. The first man that comes in this hall, why, he's going to get it."

When the Legionnaires burst in, Everest and other Wobblies fired. Three Legionnaires fell dead. The other Wobblies were immediately arrested but Everest ran from the hall and into the woods.

A mob followed and trapped him in the middle of a river. Knowing he would be lynched, Everest fired again. A fourth Legionnaire was slain.

When Everest's gun was empty the mob swarmed over him, beating out his teeth with a rifle butt. "You haven't the guts to hang a man in the daytime," he said. He was right. He was taken to the jail, but that night the mob came back. "Tell the boys I died for my class," said Everest as he was dragged out.

Everest was mutilated, then driven to a railroad bridge. The lynchers hanged him with three different ropes before they let him die. Then they riddled his body with bullets.

No one was ever punished for the murder. The coroner's report said, "Everest broke out of jail, went to the . . . bridge, and committed suicide. He jumped off with a rope around his neck and then shot himself full of holes."

Press and political reaction was predictable. One headline said: RETURNED HEROES SLAIN BY IWW. A congressman announced that the Legionnaires were "victims of a . . . conspiracy to bring about an armed revolution in the United States."

Both Congress and the press did all they could to keep America's nerves on edge. A committee headed by Senator Lee Overman investigated the Bolshevik threat. Instead of finding it largely a myth the Overman committee concluded that revolution was about to break loose at any moment. It recommended a peacetime sedition law and more anti-Bolshevik propaganda.

In New York, a state legislative committee headed by Clayton R. Lusk also investigated the Bolshevik threat. Lusk authorized a series of raids on radical and immigrant organizations. Then he announced that Bolsheviks were everywhere, especially in the unions. He proposed a number of anti-radical laws, including one requiring all schoolteachers to take a loyalty oath.

The press issued its own scare stories on the Bolsheviks. One reporter wrote that there were five million Reds in the country plus another 10 to 15 million sympathizers.

As fear and hysteria mounted, so did the demand

for action. President Wilson's administration kept pressing for a new sedition law. But though the Senate passed one it got stalled in the House of Representatives.

Meanwhile, 37 state legislatures passed their own laws against sedition or syndicalism or both. Thirty-two states also outlawed the red flag, the symbol of revolution. Because of these laws, unpopular ideas were still criminal. Free speech had little meaning. During 1919 and 1920 some 1,400 persons were arrested for violating state sedition, syndicalist, or red flag legislation.

In Washington, A. Mitchell Palmer, the new Attorney General, watched the frenzy with mounting frustration. Palmer was a Pennsylvania Quaker who had supported liberal causes. When he took office in March 1919, there was hope he might be more concerned about civil liberties than Thomas Gregory, the man he succeeded.

Perhaps he might have been, but the bombing of his own home in June may have convinced him there really was a Red menace. More important, he wanted to be President.

The elections of 1920 were in sight. Americans were in the grip of a Red Scare. The man who put down the Bolshevik threat might easily be swept into the White House.

There was place for someone to emerge as the nation's savior because the country was without a leader. In October 1919, President Wilson suffered a stroke. He was too sick to rule and too stubborn to re-

*J. Edgar Hoover in his early days as head of the Justice Department's anti-radical division.*

sign. For the next 17 months the country really had no President. The few decisions that came out of the sickroom in the White House were made by Mrs. Wilson.

Since there was room at the top, Palmer decided to move up. The Justice Department already had a Bureau of Investigation. In August, Palmer established an anti-radical division within the bureau. J. Edgar Hoover, then 24 years old, was placed in charge.

Hoover set up a card file with the names of known or suspected radicals, their organizations and publications. By Hoover's count, there were some 60,000 dangerous radicals in America. Nine out of every ten were aliens.

If these figures were correct the solution to the Red Scare and Palmer's ambitions were one. There was still no peacetime sedition law but there was the Deportation Act of 1918. Palmer would use this law to end the Red threat by cleansing the country of its alien radicals.

Thus an order went out from the Bureau of Investigation to all of its agents. "In the present state of the Federal law," it read, "investigation should be particularly directed to persons not citizens of the United States, with a view of obtaining deportation cases."

## 15

# The Fighting Quaker

*Those who can not or will not live the life of Americans . . . should go back to the countries from which they came.*

A. Mitchell Palmer

What was later called the "deportations delirium" began in the Northwest. After the general strike in

Seattle the Justice Department sent 54 aliens east on a train nicknamed the "Red Special." When they reached the coast they were to be deported.

The move ran into criticism and legal problems, and only three of the aliens were actually shipped out of the country. But this was the spring of 1919. By the fall the nation was howling for more "Red Specials" and more deportations. Attorney General Palmer was eager to oblige.

On November 7 and 8 came the cross-country raids on the Union of Russian Workers. This was when hundreds of aliens were arrested in one weekend. Literature was seized, property was wrecked, and foreign heads were broken. Many Americans cheered. They finally had the action they wanted.

As a result of the raids on the Union of Russian Workers and other radical roundups, 249 aliens were found to be eligible for deportation. J. Edgar Hoover took care of the details. He obtained the use of an army transport, the *Buford*, and invited certain congressmen to New York to see the boat off.

Twelve of the aliens aboard had to leave their families behind. At one point some wives and children attempted to break through the gates to sail with them. This was reported by the press as: REDS STORM FERRY GATES TO FREE PALS. Other wives did not know what had happened to their husbands until after the ship had gone.

When the *Buford* sailed on December 21, the press and public roared their approval. Newspapers gleefully named the boat the "Soviet Ark." "Let there be more deportations," begged one daily. A minister suggested that alien radicals be deported "in ships of stone with sails of lead." But the famous preacher Billy Sunday disagreed. "I would stand them up before a firing squad," he said, "and save space on our ships."

As a result of the November raids and the sailing of the *Buford*, A. Mitchell Palmer became a hero. He was called the "Fighting Quaker" and "a tower of strength." Obviously he was on the right road to the White House. Soon J. Edgar Hoover announced there would be a second, third, and as many more Soviet Arks as necessary.

Having made this commitment, the Justice Department had to find the cargo. Palmer knew where to look. Late in the summer of 1919 American radicals had founded the Communist Party and the Communist Labor Party. Two separate groups were necessary because, in the manner of radicals, America's Communists already disagreed on policy even before they had a chance to make it.

Together the two Communist parties had no more than 40,000 members. Most of them were former Socialists who were guilty of nothing more than dull and exaggerated rhetoric. But Palmer saw the groups as armies of the domestic revolution. Since many of the members were aliens he decided to use the Deportation Act of 1918 to get rid of them.

He laid his trap carefully. First he had undercover agents of the Justice Department infiltrate various branches of the two parties.

*Attorney General Palmer believed radicals should look the part. "Out of the sly and crafty eyes of many of them," he wrote, "leap cupidity, cruelty, insanity, and crime. From their lopsided faces, sloping brows, and misshapen features may be recognized the unmistakable criminal type." Above, Palmer (in white suit) and three aides. Above right, four anarchists.*

Then he made certain he had the cooperation of the Labor Department. For there was one curious flaw in Palmer's crusade. The Justice Department could not deport aliens. They were the responsibility of the Secretary of Labor and only he had the right to expel them.

The Secretary of Labor was a former coal miner named William B. Wilson. This Wilson was too lib-

eral for Palmer's taste. So was the Assistant Secretary, Louis F. Post. But while William Wilson was ill and Post was busy, Palmer won the support of several other members of the Labor Department. They agreed with him that membership in either of the Communist parties made an alien deportable, although only the Secretary of Labor could make such a ruling. They also agreed to change the rules for deportation hearings.

Deportation was not a criminal procedure. It involved neither judge nor jury. An unwanted alien was given a hearing before an immigration official. If the official decided against him, the alien could appeal to the Secretary of Labor. In certain cases the alien could appeal to a federal court.

If Palmer had evidence of crimes by specific aliens he could take them to court for trial. But he had no such evidence. The Justice Department, after months spent investigating the bombings of May and June, had found no suspects. Thus the only way Palmer could get rid of aliens was to deport them for their ideas rather than for crimes he couldn't seem to prove.

Even so, Palmer was afraid aliens who had legal help might escape. Therefore his allies in the Labor Department changed the rules for his benefit. An alien no longer had to be told he could have a lawyer until the deportation hearing had "proceeded sufficiently in the development of the facts to protect the Government's interests."

Since most aliens were terrified of authority and spoke little English, it was easy to get them to admit to anything if no one was there to advise them of their rights. Palmer later complained that a hearing held with a lawyer present "got us nowhere."

When he was through, Palmer had unbalanced the scales so that aliens had no chance. He did not want justice; he wanted headlines.

On December 27, 1919, secret orders were issued by the Justice Department to district chiefs. The orders revealed the "date fixed for the arrests of the COMMUNISTS is Friday evening, January 2, 1920."

There were several pages of instructions. Arrests were to be made between 7 P.M. that night and 7 A.M. the following morning. This was so aliens could be caught at public meetings or in their beds, without a way to escape or to summon a lawyer.

Secrecy was essential. If agents needed the assistance of local police "such assistance should not be requested until a few hours before the time set for the arrests, in order that no 'leak' may occur."

To trap the aliens, undercover agents who had infiltrated the Communist parties were to call meetings for the date set. This way federal agents could just walk into the meeting halls and make their arrests.

Meeting rooms were to be searched for membership lists. Agents were also told that "all literature, books, papers and anything hanging on the walls should be gathered up." In addition all aliens were to be "thoroughly searched."

The purpose of the raids was to arrest aliens. But if U.S. citizens were found at the meetings they were to be turned over to local authorities. Then they could be prosecuted under state sedition or syndicalist laws.

Agents were ordered to arrest first and find evidence later. "Every effort should be made by you," said the instructions, "to definitely establish the fact that the persons arrested are members of either the COMMUNIST PARTY of America or the COMMUNIST LABOR PARTY." This was necessary because "grounds for deportation in these cases will be based solely upon membership" in either of the Communist parties.

The Bureau of Investigation would be open all night on January 2. If agents had problems they were to check with J. Edgar Hoover. The morning after the raids agents were to send Hoover, by special delivery, a complete list of the persons arrested, the organization they belonged to, and a note about whether there had been warrants for them.

A warrant is a legal order authorizing an officer of the law to make an arrest, or search or seize property. Warrants are supposed to be issued before, not after, arrests or searches are made. But the Bureau of Investigation was prepared to do its work illegally. The instructions cautioned that "where arrests are made of persons not covered by warrants," agents should request them as soon as possible. But warrants or not, arrests were to be made.

Agents were also to telegraph Hoover "the total number of persons of each organization taken into custody, together with a statement of any interesting evidence secured."

The same day this letter went out, one of Palmer's allies in the Labor Department signed more than 3,000 warrants for the arrest of aliens known to be members of either of the Communist parties.

A dragnet is a net that is dragged along the bottom of a stream in the hope of catching a fish. The Justice Department was ready to throw out a dragnet in the hope that among all the innocent people trapped there might be some deportable aliens.

# 16

# Night of Terror

*This . . . seems to have been conducted under that modern
theory of statesmanship that you hang first and try after-
wards.*

Judge George W. Anderson

If the years between 1917 and 1920 were America's
Reign of Terror, January 2, 1920, was America's
night of terror. In a series of dramatic raids more than
4,000 persons were arrested in 33 cities.

The undercover agents did their work well. They
managed to arrange for many Communist party clubs
to meet that night. Where these meetings were in
progress, federal agents just barged in and arrested
everyone present.

But the agents did not limit themselves to meeting
places. They went wherever alien radicals were believed to gather, including restaurants, pool halls,
bowling alleys, and certain schools.

As instructed, wherever agents broke in they
searched for membership lists. When such lists were
found the agents went hunting for the people in their
homes. In this way many persons were pulled out of
bed in the dead of night to be taken to prison.

Meeting rooms and homes were searched without
warrants. Everything visible was either seized or
smashed. In New Jersey, the raiders found some
drawings they thought were diagrams of a bomb.
They turned out to be diagrams of a phonograph. In

*Victims of the Palmer raids: a few of the more than 4,000 men and women arrested in one night of terror. Under armed guard they are boarding a steamer for Ellis Island in New York harbor.*

Massachusetts, agents ripped down a suspicious-looking sign in Russian. It said: "No Smoking."

Wherever they struck, agents arrested everything on two legs. In Newark, New Jersey, a man was seized on the street because he "looked like a radical." People were arrested because agents decided they were on their way to a suspicious meeting or school. Bystanders who made the mistake of asking what was happening were also picked up.

Most of the arrests were made without warrants. When the prisoners were in custody the agents tried to match their names against the warrants they had on hand. In some places not a single prisoner matched a single warrant.

Because of the nature of the raids there were the usual abuses.

In Chelsea, Massachusetts, Mrs. Stanislas Vasiliewska was at a meeting with her 13-year-old daughter. Both mother and child were thrown into jail.

In Lynn, Massachusetts, agents burst into a meeting and arrested 39 men. It was later discovered they had gathered to discuss plans to organize a cooperative bakery. After spending the night in jail, 38 of the men were released. Only one had happened to be a Communist, and he was a U.S. citizen.

In Boston, Minnie Federman woke at 6 A.M. to find six or seven agents in her bedroom. She had to dress in a closet while the agents ripped open her mattress and searched the apartment. After several hours in the police station she was freed. She was neither a radical nor an alien.

All over America people were swept into prison without warning. They were not permitted to notify family, friends, or lawyers. Men and women disappeared without anyone knowing where or why. Families were left without fathers to support them.

Bail in immigration cases was usually only $500. Now it was set as high as $10,000. The Justice Department did not want any of the prisoners freed to see lawyers before they could be questioned. J. Edgar

Hoover said that permitting aliens to have legal advice "defeats the ends of justice."

Palmer, Hoover, and their men had given so much thought to arresting as many persons as possible that they had no time to consider what would be done with them afterward.

About half of the prisoners in the New England area were sent to Deer Island in Boston Harbor. Their cells had no heat, even though it was January. The cots had no blankets or mattresses. One prisoner killed himself, another went mad, and others died of pneumonia.

In Detroit, some 800 men and boys were herded into a dark, narrow, windowless corridor in a federal building. They had to step over each other to move about. At night they slept on the bare stone floor.

There were only one water fountain and one toilet for all 800 prisoners. For the first 20 hours they were fed nothing. Afterward they were given food brought by relatives and friends.

It took three days before the Detroit authorities began to sort out their victims. By the end of the sixth day 350 of the prisoners had been released for lack of evidence.

About 140 of those still in custody were transferred to another building. On the way, their pictures were taken by newspaper photographers. When the photos appeared the prisoners looked like everyone's vision of a Bolshevik—dirty, wrinkled, unshaven, uncombed. Of course Palmer and Hoover would have looked the same if they had been forced to sleep on

*Hyman Kaplan, an alien living in Lawrence, Massachusetts, was awakened and arrested at home in the middle of the night, while his children slept. He was first taken to Boston and then imprisoned in a freezing cell on Deer Island.*

the floor for a week without bathing or shaving.

But Palmer could not be bothered by such details as suffering and injustice. All in all he was quite content with the raids. He said he had "halted the advance of 'red radicalism' in the United States" and was "sweeping the nation clean of . . . alien filth." Then he sat back to wait for the cheers and votes of a grateful people.

# 17

# The Morning After

*As a rule, the hearings show the aliens arrested to be working men of good character who have never been arrested before, who are not anarchists or revolutionists, nor politically or otherwise dangerous in any sense.*

Louis F. Post

At first there were loud cheers. The press and public were so eager to believe the nation had been saved from a dreadful fate they were willing to overlook the manner in which it had been done. "There is no time to waste on hair-splitting over infringement of liberty," wrote the *Washington Post.*

But amid the applause there was a low sound of hissing. It grew louder as Americans began to realize all that had happened on the night of January 2. For Palmer had made the fatal error of all demagogues. He had overreached himself. He had violated too many rights and arrested too many innocent people. Many Americans took a second look at what had happened and began to wonder who would be the next victim.

Every nation has a right to decide which foreigners to admit. It also has a right to decide which to deport. But while aliens live in America they have the same basic rights as anyone else. The Bill of Rights protects the liberties of "people" and "persons," not just citizens.

Many Americans had originally fled from Europe to escape the terror of a knock on the door in the

middle of the night, arrest without warrant, imprison-
ment without trial. These were the marks of tyranny,
not democracy.

The Palmer raids helped shock Americans into a
return to common sense and common decency. So
did the excesses of the New York state legislature. On
January 7, a few days after the raids, the legislature
refused to seat five of its members because they were
Socialists.

The Socialist Party was legal in New York. It had
the right to run candidates for office. The men had
been fairly elected by the voters of their districts. Yet
they were denied their places because there no longer
seemed to be room in America for a minority point of
view.

The year before, the same thing had happened in
Washington. The House of Representatives refused
to seat a Socialist who had been elected in Wisconsin.
These two incidents disturbed even the most conservative Americans. Would the day come when Democrats refused to seat Republicans, or Republicans refused to seat Democrats, because they did not agree?

The Palmer raids and the action of the New York
state legislature marked the peak of the Red Scare.
From then on it ran downhill. For the first time since
the Espionage Act was passed in 1917, civil liberties
became the concern of many, not just a few.

It became clear that if the rights of small groups
continued to be violated, the rights of larger groups
would follow. Soon there would be no right left at all
—except the right to agree with whoever was in
power.

The drive for a peacetime sedition law collapsed, as different groups turned against it. Many people realized that what had happened to aliens during the Palmer raids might happen to U.S. citizens under such a law. Newspapers began to worry less about increasing circulation through scare headlines and more about freedom of the press.

As the concern for civil liberties mounted, so did the concern for the victims of the Palmer raids. Of over 4,000 arrested, some 1,300 were released for lack of evidence. If there was no cause even to arrest one-third of the prisoners, there was good reason to question the methods of the Justice Department.

Attorney General Palmer, his eye still on the White House, announced boldly that at least 2,700 persons would be deported as a result of the raids. But there were some Americans who cared about justice even if the head of the Justice Department was not one of them.

Palmer's first major setback came from Louis F. Post, the Assistant Secretary of Labor. Because Labor Secretary Wilson was ill, Post became Acting Secretary. In this capacity he had to decide whether or not the arrested aliens should be deported.

Post was a crusty, 71-year-old liberal with strong opinions about civil liberties. After examining the evidence he reached some conclusions that undid most of Palmer's work.

Post decided that most of the men arrested were not criminals. They were honest laborers who would make good American citizens.

He accepted recent court rulings that evidence seized illegally could not be used against a defendant.

He said aliens had a right to a lawyer before they were questioned.

He also said that being on a membership list did not make a man a Communist. Many aliens did not even know what communism was all about. They were listed as members because they had belonged to other organizations which had merged into the Communist Party.

Finally, Post ruled that an alien could not be deported unless there was proof he had done or said something that showed he was aware of the character of the Communist Party.

Late in January 1920, Secretary of Labor Wilson had ruled that membership in the Communist Party was a deportable offense. But in May he ruled that membership in the Communist Labor Party was not a deportable offense. There was really very little difference between the two parties. What was different was that in January the hysteria had been at its height and in May it was dying.

By the time Post and Wilson were through with their rulings, over 2,000 deportation warrants had been canceled. In the end some 550 aliens were found to be deportable.

The Justice Department once boasted it had the names of over 60,000 radicals on J. Edgar Hoover's little Red list. Ninety percent of them, or some 54,000, were aliens.

For all their sleuthing and posturing and abuses

Palmer and Hoover had found and arrested about one percent of the men they said were dangerous. By any standards it was a poor showing.

An angry Palmer blamed his failures on Louis Post. He demanded that Post be fired for his "perverted sympathy for the criminal anarchists of the country."

A House committee investigated Post, but he was not cowed. He demanded the opportunity to defend himself. When it was granted, Post calmly explained to the congressmen how the Justice Department was breaking the law rather than enforcing it.

Then he added, "It is unfair . . . to the country to assume everybody whom a detective charges with culpability shall, therefore, be deported, and whoever stands in the way, no matter how wisely he may do it . . . shall be denounced as a defender of Reds."

The charges against Post were dropped. Before long it would be Palmer who would be called on to justify his actions before Congress and the nation.


## 18

# The Quaking Fighter

*There is no danger of revolution so great as that created by suppression, by ruthlessness, and by deliberate violation of the simple rules of American law and American decency.*

National Popular Government League


Palmer had to fend off several major assaults in the

spring of 1920. One of the most damaging was a report issued by the National Popular Government League.

The League was a reform group founded in 1913. It aimed to "democratize our political machinery, and establish the control of government by the people."

The League was outraged by Palmer's behavior. So was the National Civil Liberties Bureau, which had been fighting a rather lonely battle against government oppression for almost three years.

Early in 1920 the Bureau reorganized and took its present name, the American Civil Liberties Union (ACLU). Together, the ACLU and the National Popular Government League decided to investigate and document the abuses committed by the Justice Department.

Their report was issued by the League in May 1920. It was signed by 12 of the most important lawyers in the country. All of them had supported the war and some had been important government officials. It was just not possible to question their integrity or their patriotism.

The report used case histories to demonstrate how Palmer had violated the Bill of Rights.

The Fourth Amendment says, "The right of the people to be secure in their persons, houses, papers, and effects, against unreasonable searches and seizures, shall not be violated, and no warrants shall issue but upon probable cause." Yet homes, halls, and people had been searched unreasonably and without warrants. Many persons were arrested without warrants, and many warrants were issued without "probable cause."

The Fifth Amendment says, "No person . . . shall be compelled . . . to be a witness against himself, nor be deprived of life, liberty, or property, without due process of law." Yet aliens were forced, by threats or beatings, to give evidence which could be used against them. Many attempts were made to deprive them of liberty and property without due process of law.

The Eighth Amendment says, "Excessive bail shall not be required . . . nor cruel and unusual punishments inflicted." Yet many aliens had their bail deliberately set higher than they could pay. Cruel and unusual punishments were inflicted both by the agents who beat them and by the conditions under which they were imprisoned.

The report also criticized the use of undercover agents. Such spies often acted as provocative agents, recruiting members for the Communist parties and writing their material. These agents also served to trap the Communists by calling meetings for the night of January 2. This entrapment violated the spirit of the First Amendment, which guarantees the right "peaceably to assemble."

Finally, the report attacked Palmer for his propaganda activities. He had used government funds to prepare and distribute anti-radical cartoons and articles to the newspapers in order to make the Red menace seem greater and to justify his acts. The report called this "an advertising campaign in favor of repression."

*A 1920 cartoon mocked A. Mitchell Palmer's agents. The drawing pretends to be a fashion note about a "Palmer Sleuthing Coat, worn with gumshoes and false whiskers."*

Palmer suffered another sharp blow when 18 of the aliens arrested in the Boston area took their case to federal court. The trial, which was known as *Colyer v. Skeffington,* took place in the spring of 1920. It showed the extent to which the Justice Department had trampled over human rights.

In the course of the trial, every illegal act became a matter of public record. The secret instructions to bureau chiefs were revealed. Agents were forced to admit they had made arrests and seized material without warrants.

As he listened to the testimony, Judge George W. Anderson was shocked. At one point he said of the raids, "A more lawless proceeding it is hard for anybody to conceive!"

Yet all of this criticism did not hurt Palmer as much as he hurt himself. In March he had announced that he was a candidate for President. But he soon realized the public was getting skeptical or bored with his anti-Red crusade.

Palmer decided to make a dramatic attempt to revive both the crusade and his political hopes. He declared that the Reds would rise on May 1. J. Edgar Hoover and his sleuths warned there would be strikes, bombings, assassinations.

Once again the old trick worked. Hysteria flared as preparations were made to combat the revolution. In New York, police were put on 24-hour duty. In Boston, trucks with mounted machine guns were parked at strategic locations. In Chicago, 360 suspected radicals were thrown in jail for the day. Everywhere, important persons and places were heavily guarded.

May 1 dawned and departed. Nothing happened. There were no riots, no bombs, no murders.

Now Americans felt they had been made fools of. They turned on Palmer with the deadliest weapon known to any demagogue. They laughed at him. The "Fighting Quaker" became known as the "Quaking Fighter."

Even Congress was annoyed. Palmer was summoned first to a House and then to a Senate hearing. "I apologize for nothing that the Department of Justice has done," he told the senators. "I glory in it."

But no one else gloried in it. People were tired of being afraid without reason. Although the Bolsheviks had taken firm control in Russia, they had been turned back everywhere else in Europe. In America they had never shown any serious signs of life. The Red threat was more imaginary than real. Palmer had done more harm to American democracy than any radical, alien or domestic.

By the fall of 1920 the Red Scare was scarcely a shiver. On September 16, a wagonload of bombs exploded on Wall Street in New York City, the hub of American capitalism. Thirty-three persons were killed

*The Wall Street bombing of September 1920 may have been aimed at capitalists, but all of its victims were workers. The Bureau of Investigation never found out who was responsible for the crime.*

and over 200 were injured. It was far more serious than all of the bombings of 1919 put together.

Palmer raced to New York and again announced the revolution was at hand. This time most people yawned. When the Bureau of Investigation, with its customary skill, failed to find any suspects, people snickered. One newspaper said of Palmer's claims, "The usual pinch of salt must be used."

The old anti-Red cries had worn themselves out. They had been used too often. People turned their attention to the Presidential campaign of 1920. Newspapers began to devote their headlines to baseball scandals, illegal liquor, movie stars, and short skirts.

America's Reign of Terror was over.

## 19

# Back to Normal

*America's present need is not heroics but healing; not nostrums but normalcy.*

Warren G. Harding

When the Terror died so did Palmer's chance of becoming President in 1920. The Democrats nominated Governor James M. Cox of Ohio. The Republicans nominated Senator Warren G. Harding, also of Ohio.

The Red Scare was so stale that neither side made it a campaign issue. Harding commented that "too much has been said about Bolshevism in America."

He called for a return to "normalcy."

The people answered his call. Harding got 16 million votes; Cox got only 9 million. Millions of Democrats, disgusted with Woodrow Wilson, deserted their party. One liberal said Wilson had put "his enemies in office and his friends in jail." After three years of persecution, liberals and voters of foreign origin either turned to Harding or stayed home on Election Day.

Some 915,302 voters showed their sentiments another way. They cast their ballots for prisoner Number 9653 in the federal prison at Atlanta, Georgia. He was the Socialist Party candidate, Eugene Debs.

As soon as Harding took office, the ACLU and other groups began to press him to free Debs and the other political prisoners. Wilson was so rigidly principled he had no room for compassion. Harding was much less principled but much more kind. He freed Debs on Christmas Day, 1921.

The *New York Times* and the American Legion protested. "Certainly the majority will not approve," scolded the *Times.*

But Harding continued to free those imprisoned under the Espionage and Sedition Acts. When the President died in August 1923, he was succeeded by another conservative Republican, Calvin Coolidge. Coolidge freed virtually all of the remaining political prisoners by the end of that year.

Although the Terror and the Red Scare were dead, so was reform. Big business ran the country. "Never before, here or anywhere else, has a government been

*Eugene Debs, after being notified that the Socialist Party had chosen him to run for President of the United States in 1920. Although World War I had been over for two years, Debs was still in prison for opposing it.*

so completely fused with business," wrote the *Wall Street Journal.*

There was no longer any dramatic persecution of unpopular ideas because it was not necessary. The leading radical organizations had been crippled or destroyed. Yet a quieter persecution persisted.

The American Legion and other self-styled super-patriotic groups kept their vigil over public opinion. They still insisted that the schools, churches, and unions were havens for Bolsheviks. As a result of their pressure many states forced schoolteachers to take loyalty oaths and textbooks were banned or rewritten.

Loss of a job or income can be as terrifying a punishment as prison or the whip. Those with independent ideas learned there was safety in silence. To a great extent people lost their interest in politics.

The Justice Department also continued to harass people for their opinions and to break unions and strikes. Finally, in 1924, President Coolidge's Attorney General, Harlan Stone, decided it was time to clean up.

He wanted no more political persecution and no more Palmer raids. Yet the man he chose to reorganize the Bureau of Investigation was the architect of the raids, J. Edgar Hoover.

Hoover blamed the raids on his superiors and said he had played an "unwilling part." In January 1925, J. Edgar Hoover began his lifetime career as director of what would later be called the Federal Bureau of Investigation (FBI).

While the shadow of the Terror still fell across many American citizens, it almost put out the lamp held by the Statue of Liberty. New laws were passed to limit the number of immigrants who could come to America. A national-origins quota was put into effect restricting the number of immigrants who could enter from each country.

The national-origins quota favored the people of western Europe. The unwanted flood of immigration from southern and eastern Europe was narrowed to a trickle.

Hatred of aliens and radicals continued to fester long after "normalcy" had returned. In May 1920, two Italian anarchists were arrested in Brockton, Massachusetts. They were accused of taking part in a payroll robbery in which two men were murdered.

*End of an Era: the funeral procession in Boston for Sacco and Vanzetti.*

Nicola Sacco and Bartolomeo Vanzetti were tried in 1921 and found guilty. The evidence was doubtful. What was beyond doubt, however, was that the judge and jury were prejudiced against the defendants because they were aliens, Italians, and anarchists.

For six years lawyers and liberals fought for a new trial for the two men. It was never granted. In August 1927, Sacco and Vanzetti were executed.

The Terror had claimed its last two victims.

# Epilogue

*It is not enough to allow dissent. We must demand it. For there is much to dissent from.*

Robert F. Kennedy

More than half a century has passed since the Terror. It is an almost forgotten period of American history. Few people have heard of the Palmer raids. Even fewer recall the years of persecution that preceded them.

Of all the major figures involved, history has been kindest to Woodrow Wilson. He is honored for championing the League of Nations and for saying the right things often and well. He is rarely remembered as the President who came closest to destroying free expression in America.

The purpose of the Terror was to crush dissent and

reform. In that sense it succeeded only temporarily. Both dissent and reform eventually rose from the ashes and the fight for a better life went on. As a result much has been achieved in the past fifty years. But much more remains to be done.

More Americans earn more money than ever before. But millions still live and die in poverty.

Most labor unions have won the struggle for existence. Some have become as powerful as big business. But many of the migrant laborers and farm workers the IWW tried to help are still unorganized, unrecognized, or exploited.

The national-origins quota for immigrants has been abolished. Immigrants from southern and eastern Europe are no longer discriminated against. But aliens can still be barred or deported because of their views.

Blacks are rarely lynched any more. But the struggle for equality in employment, education, housing, justice, and political power goes on.

More people care about civil liberties than ever before, but more people have been spied upon than ever before. The FBI still polices political opinion, is indifferent to civil liberties, and often mistakes reform for rebellion. Radicals and reformers are still persecuted. The American Legion still worries about the loyalty of schoolteachers.

The Sedition Act of 1918 has been repealed. But there is still an Espionage Act punishing "false reports or false statements" in wartime. There is also a peacetime sedition act which is primarily aimed at members of the Communist Party.

For communism remains the nightmare that haunts the American dream. In periods of calm some Americans still use the old Red Scare technique of labeling anything they dislike Communist. In periods of crisis this can again become a national mania.

In many ways the early 1950s were like the period that followed World War I. America was exhausted by another major war, World War II. She was involved in a small but dirty war in Korea. The enemies were Communists; communism seemed to be expanding across the globe.

At home prices were soaring and there were many strikes. Instead of imaginary spies there were real ones who were found guilty of giving atomic secrets to Russia.

Americans became confused and suspicious. A senator from Wisconsin, Joseph R. McCarthy, saw his chance, just as A. Mitchell Palmer had earlier.

McCarthy began flinging reckless charges of communism in all directions. Others took up the cry. It was the Red Scare all over again, except that this time many of the victims were high government officials rather than unknown aliens. Lives were ruined, careers were destroyed, dissent and reform were smothered.

Like all demagogues, McCarthy destroyed himself by going too far. But though McCarthy is dead, McCarthyism lives on. It stands for many things. One of them is the belief that criticism is equal to treason.

The danger of McCarthyism, Palmerism, or Wilsonism is that when criticism is suppressed, so is truth. Wilson was so certain he was right about World War I that he sent his critics to jail. But the war neither ended all wars nor made the world safe for democracy. History proved the critics were right and Wilson was wrong.

During the war in Vietnam, Americans who disagreed with government policy were repeatedly accused of betraying their country. But in time the government adopted some of the views and proposals of its critics. The course of the war was changed by dissenters who had the courage to speak out.

Free speech is essential not because it is pleasant to be criticized, but because the other person may be right. Unless he can be heard there is no way of knowing.

One of the chief differences between America and the totalitarian nations is the Bill of Rights. It is the Bill of Rights that guarantees free speech, free press, a fair trial, and everything else that means justice and freedom. It is the Bill of Rights that protects the individual from the great power of the government. There is no such protection in a totalitarian state.

Democracy cannot be preserved by violating the Bill of Rights. It can only be destroyed.

The answer to violent radicalism is peaceful progress, for it is impossible to lead a rebellion against a just society. The answer to totalitarian communism and to fascism is not to imitate them, but to build a more perfect democracy.

# Bibliography

Allen, Frederick Lewis. *Only Yesterday: An Informal History of the 1920's.* Perennial Library, 1964.
———. *The Big Change, 1900-1950.* Bantam Books, 1961.
Auerbach, Frank. *Immigration Laws of the United States (2nd ed.).* Bobbs-Merrill, 1961.
Brissenden, Paul. *The I.W.W.: A Study of American Syndicalism.* Russell & Russell, 1957.
Brooks, Thomas. *Toil and Trouble: A History of American Labor.* Delta Books, 1964.
Chafee, Zechariah, Jr. *Free Speech in the United States.* Atheneum, 1969.
Coben, Stanley. *A. Mitchell Palmer: Politician.* Columbia University Press, 1963.
Creel, George. *How We Advertised America.* Harper, 1920.
Dorsen, Norman. *Frontiers of Civil Liberties.* Pantheon, 1968.
Dos Passos, John. *U.S.A.* Houghton Mifflin, 1930.
Dunn, Robert (ed.). *The Palmer Raids.* International Publishers, 1948.
Eastman, Max. *Love and Revolution.* Random House, 1964.
Farrell, John. *Beloved Lady: A History of Jane Addams' Ideas on Reform and Peace.* Johns Hopkins Press, 1967.
Feuerlicht, Roberta S. *The Desperate Act: The Assassination of Franz Ferdinand at Sarajevo.* McGraw-Hill, 1968.
Ginger, Ray. *Eugene V. Debs.* Collier Books, 1962.
Handlin, Oscar (ed.). *Immigration as a Factor in American History.* Prentice-Hall, 1959.
Higham, John. *Strangers in the Land: Patterns of American Nativism, 1860–1925.* Atheneum, 1968.
Horowitz, Irving (ed.). *The Anarchists.* Laurel Books, 1964.
Hyman, Harold. *To Try Men's Souls: Loyalty Tests in American History.* University of California Press, 1959.
Johnson, Donald. *The Challenge to American Freedoms: World War I and the Rise of the American Civil Liberties Union.* University of Kentucky Press, 1963.
———. "The Political Career of A. Mitchell Palmer." *Pennsylvania History,* October 1958.

Kornbluh, Joyce. *Rebel Voices: An I.W.W. Anthology.* University of Michigan Press, 1964.

Lecar, Helene. *The Russian Revolution.* Ardmore Press, 1967.

Leuchtenburg, William. *The Perils of Prosperity, 1914–1932.* University of Chicago Press, 1958.

Link, Arthur. *Woodrow Wilson and the Progressive Era, 1910–1917.* Harper Torchbook, 1963.

Lowenthal, Max. *The Federal Bureau of Investigation.* William Sloane, 1950.

Mandelbaum, Seymour. *The Social Setting of Intolerance.* Scott, Foresman, 1964.

Milner, Lucille. "Freedom of Speech in Wartime." *New Republic,* November 25, 1940.

Mitchell, David. *1919: Red Mirage.* Macmillan, 1970.

Mock, James, and Cedric Larson. *Words That Won the War: The Story of the Committee on Public Information, 1917–1919.* Princeton University Press, 1939.

Mowry, George (ed.). *The Twenties.* Prentice-Hall, 1963.

Murray, Robert. *Red Scare: A Study of National Hysteria, 1919–1920.* McGraw-Hill Paperback, 1964.

*New Republic.* "The Red Hysteria." January 28, 1920.

Panunzio, Constantine. *The Deportation Cases of 1919–1920.* Federal Council of Churches of Christ in America, 1921.

Post, Louis F. *The Deportations Delirium of 1920.* Charles H. Kerr, 1923.

Preston, William, Jr. *Aliens and Dissenters: Federal Suppression of Radicals, 1903–1933.* Harper Torchbook, 1966.

Rayback, Joseph. *A History of American Labor.* Free Press Paperback, 1966.

Renshaw, Patrick. *The Wobblies.* Anchor Books, 1968.

*Report upon the Illegal Practices of the United States Department of Justice by Twelve Lawyers.* National Popular Government League, 1920.

Slosson, Preston. *The Great Crusade and After, 1914–1928.* Macmillan, 1930.

Smith, Gene. *When the Cheering Stopped: The Last Years of Woodrow Wilson.* Morrow, 1964.

Spinrad, William. *Civil Liberties.* Quadrangle Books, 1970.

Taylor, A. J. P. *A History of the First World War.* Berkley Medallion Books, 1966.

Tuchman, Barbara. *The Guns of August.* Dell, 1963.

————. *The Proud Tower: A Portrait of the World before the War, 1890–1914.* Macmillan, 1966.

Tuttle, William M., Jr. *Race Riot: Chicago in the Red Summer of 1919.* Atheneum, 1970.

Waskow, Arthur. *From Race Riot to Sit-In: 1919 and the 1960's.* Anchor Books, 1967.

# Index

ROBERTA STRAUSS FEUERLICHT's fourteen books
for young people include an account of how World War I
began (*The Desperate Act*), a book about the Nobel Peace
Prize (*In Search of Peace*), and a biography of Henry VIII.
Mrs. Feuerlicht lives in New York City.

NORMAN DORSEN is professor of law at New York University, general counsel of the American Civil Liberties
Union, and editor of *The Rights of Americans: What They
Are, What They Should Be.*